Light from the Dark Valley

Light from the Dark Valley

Reflections on Suffering and the Care of the Dying

SHEILA CASSIDY

DARTON·LONGMAN + TODD

First published in 1994 by
Darton, Longman and Todd Ltd
1 Spencer Court
140–142 Wandsworth High Street
London SW18 4JJ

Reprinted 1994

ISBN 0–232–52055–0

A catalogue record for this book is available
from the British Library

Phototypeset in 10½/12½pt Baskerville by Intype, London
Printed and bound in Great Britain
by Page Bros, Norwich

To my patient theological telephone mentors, who answer questions, look up references, read manuscripts, encourage me to go on stretching my mind and heart:

Gordon Mursell
Michael Ivens SJ
Bonaventure Knollys OSB
Angela Tilby
Oliver Davies
Michael Hollings
Anthony Fisher OP
Henry Wansbrough OSB

May God reward them all with health and happiness, and, if possible, portable phones and personal fax machines so that they may be even more available to me!

And a special hug for John Wilkins, editor of *The Tablet*, who is so warm in his acceptances and gentle in his rejection of my offerings.

Contents

Acknowledgements

MY FIRST THANKS must go to those kind theologians (named in my dedication) who have supported and encouraged me over the years: I doubt I should be as patient with some foolish theologian who took it into his head to write about things medical! I am deeply grateful to Abbot David and the community of Buckfast Abbey who financed the printing of a trial run of these essays. Even kinder was the patient Alison who spent hours and hours actually copying and binding the original run of two hundred copies – she at least will be grateful to DLT for taking over the printing! Lastly my thanks are to my secretary Barbara Tappy who can read my handwriting almost better than I can myself!

Shelia Cassidy

The following chapters have previously appeared as articles or were given as addresses:

'Why Suffering?' was first published in a separate booklet by The Canterbury Press, Norwich (1993); 'Work in the Dark Valley' appeared in the *Epworth Review,* January 1993; 'The Loneliness of the Virgin', 'The Emptiness of

God' and 'The Mystery of Redemption' – three talks given at Worcester Cathedral on Good Friday 1993; 'Christ the Fireman' appeared in *The Tablet*, Easter 1993;

'How Blest the Sorrowful' in *The Beatitudes in Modern Life*, published by the Thomas More Press (1989); and 'Euthanasia' in *The Tablet*, 3 April 1993.

The author and publisher are grateful for permission to reprint these.

Thanks are also due to the following for permission to quote copyright material: Bloodaxe Books Ltd, from *Mass for Hard Times* by R. S. Thomas; Cairns Publications, from *Healing – more or less* by the Revd James E. Cotter; Dimension Books (USA), from *Disciples and Other Strangers* edited by E. J. Farrell; St Paul MultiMedia Productions UK, from *Theotokos*, 1989 Icon Book Calendar.

Introduction

THIS RATHER MOTLEY collection of 'essays' doesn't pretend to be anything more than it is: a humble offering of spiritual musings from a doctor who works with the dying. The 'dark valley' of the title is not so much a physical place as an emotional situation – the Valley of the Shadow of Death in which I work and my patients live. I am told that in medieval times, when cities were built in forest clearings, there was a space called the *limina* between the outer walls of the city and the beginning of the dark and scary forest. The dying were seen as people living in the *limina*, outside the city walls, moving towards but not yet swallowed up by the forest Those of us who work with the dying must venture into this liminal space, but we return to the security, the warmth and lights, the comforting bustle of the city. This return to the 'normal' world is vital, for the *limina* is not meant for healthy men and women, and to spend time there with its occupants is inevitably costly. Most of the time I am not aware of the cost of my work; I like the people I work with – patients, families and carers alike – and I enjoy both the challenge of waging war against disease processes and the satisfaction of helping people to cope with pain and fear. From time to time, however, I am forced to acknowledge the pain involved in being close to those whose suffering is

[xi]

so cruel. I think what hurts most is the impotence, the having to say 'I'm sorry, I can't make you better, I can't cure your wife, I can't stop her vomiting,' and even, sometimes, 'I can't take away all the pain.' It is this sitting empty-handed beside people, foolish and useless as the women standing miserably under the cross, that makes my heart ache and drives me home at night to bury myself in yet another television drama.

These essays, then, are born from the work of the past twelve years spent alongside the terminally ill. Some have appeared in print before, in a variety of journals, but it seemed worthwhile to gather them together for a wider audience. There will inevitably, I fear, be a degree of repetition, but I hope that we have reduced it to a minimum. More than anything, I hope that perhaps my own struggle to wrest some meaning out of suffering will bring some light and comfort to those whose journey takes them through similar dark places.

1

Why Suffering?

An exploration of the problem of suffering based on the book of Job

WHY ME? How could God do this to me? What have I done to deserve this? It's not fair! How can you believe in a God who lets little children be hurt, abused, killed in accidents, die of cancer? Why, why? These and so many other anguished questions lie at the heart of the Christian experience, wherever men and women find themselves confronted by pain and disaster. Such questions, of course, are not new, for they are questions for all time, for all places and for all people. Ever since the first cave-man wept in fury and powerlessness at the death of his wife, his friend, his child, men and women have been battering the heavens with their importunate and impossible questions. And the answer, of course, never comes; or rather the answers which man works out in fury and despair when God remains silent are never really satisfactory. So, why more words on the subject, and, if I may add my own *why me?*, why should I have the temerity to try to answer the ultimate questions which have defeated theologians and philosophers since time began?

Why *me?* The real answer is caught up in the person that I am, the work that I do and my personal background. Let me explain: I am a doctor who works in a hospice for men and women with terminal cancer. This means that I am confronted on a daily basis by what is called 'the problem of suffering'; and because I spend my life working alongside people in tragic circumstances I have been forced to listen not only to my own questions about the *why* of inncoent suffering, but to those of my patients and my colleagues. This does not mean by any means that I have found the answers – simply that I have lived with these questions for many years.

Also I have had an unusual personal experience of suffering. In 1975 while working as a doctor in South America I was detained for two months by the security forces for treating a wounded revolutionary. After my arrest I was held for three days in an interrogation centre where I was tortured with electric shocks during the course of one night. I then spent three weeks in solitary confinement and, after that, five weeks in a detention camp with around one hundred other women political prisoners. It was a time of great pain, loneliness and fear and has, I believe, given me some small insight into the experience of men and women who suffer powerlessness and distress of different kinds.

This then is the experiential base from which I write. Perhaps it is useful, too, to say a word about my religious background. I write as a Roman Catholic with no formal training in theology but with a certain familiarity with the Scriptures built up over three years of monastic life and ten years as an occasional preacher and religious broadcaster. My interest in religion, therefore, is not so much academic as lived; my relationship with God in prayer and in mission is the cornerstone, the foundation, the anchor of my life. It is the inspiration of all that I do, the source of whatever small light I may shed.

Lastly, it is perhaps worth saying something about the manner in which I personally relate to God, because it affects the way I choose to wrestle with the problem of suffering. I am one of those Christians whose experience of relationship is with the transcendent God, the unknown, mysterious God of the Old Testament. Mine is the God of Abraham, Isaac, Jacob and Isaiah, and as the years go by I find myself drawn deeper and deeper into the mystery of what has come to be known as the *Cloud of Unknowing*, that unfathomable, indescribable 'place' where the human spirit meets with the Unknown God.

I have a deep sense of both the IMMANENCE, the nearness, and the TRANSCENDENCE, the otherness of God, and it is precisely this experience that makes it possible for me to live peaceably with the mystery of God and his world. This is the rock upon which the small house of my faith is built, and, like a crofter's cottage, it has stood fast during many violent storms. Now that you have at least some measure of your guide, let us set out together in faith to ask for ourselves the eternal 'why' of suffering. We must remember, however, that this is a question which has perplexed both priests and people for thousands of years and that the answer which satisfies one person may seem either naïve or incomprehensible to another. Enough. Let us begin, and because we are not theologians but ordinary people, let us take a homely image: a ball of string or wool. Perhaps if we had been the first to try to unravel this problem we might have taken firmly hold of one end and unravelled it until the other end appeared. Alas, we are not the first and we are presented with a tangled mess of threads, some of them knotted, some broken, which seem irrevocably mixed up together. Like any patient knitter, all we can do is pick a thread and gently teaze it out, seeing where it leads to.

As an Old Testament lover, I would like to take a traditional approach via the Book of Job. It is not the only entrance to the maze of the problem of suffering but it is a well-trodden path and the one with which I personally am most comfortable. If you are not familiar with Job perhaps you should pause here and read it. What follows will certainly make more sense if you do, but I will try to make it intelligible anyway.

Very little is known about the writer of this book but scholars calculate that it was written about five hundred years before the birth of Christ. The idea, however, is much older, and is taken from an ancient pagan myth, no doubt wrestling as we are with the problem of innocent suffering. In essence, the story goes like this: Job was a *good* man (though not necessarily a very clever one). He was also very successful, with a large family, a flourishing business and had the respect of all who knew him. One day Satan persuades God to test Job, to see if his virtue is not really self-interest in disguise. God agrees and Job not only loses all his family but develops a dreadful illness. Desolate, Job bewails his misfortune, protesting his innocence and eventually demanding that God give an account of himself. Job asks the question we *all* ask when disaster strikes: Why me? The central portion of the book is in the form of a dialogue between Job and three of his pious friends who try to help him come to terms with his situation. Job does not find them very helpful and eventually, in desperation, demands an answer of God. Then comes the great climax of the story, for to everyone's terror and amazement, God answers from the heart of the whirlwind. The answer, however, is not what Job or anyone else had bargained for, and that's why you and I are left 2,500 years later, still trying to untangle the knots.

Rather than paraphrase Job's story which is written in the most wonderful poetry, I'd rather tell it in modern form, using a creation of my own, a sort of Job lookalike called Joanna. Now my Jo, of course, is not a real individual, but a composite person who stands for all those who suffer through no fault of their own. If Jo's story seems a little far fetched, remember that there *are* people who suffer multiple disasters and that each misfortune that happens to Jo happens every single day to different individuals. For our purposes, however, poor Jo has a lot to bear.

Like Job, Joanna is a thoroughly *good* person. She is a devout Christian who obeys all the commandments, goes to church on Sundays, says her morning and night prayers, runs the Sunday School and sings in the church choir. She arranges the flowers in church, does voluntary work at the hospital, visits prisoners and unmarried mothers and is a member of Amnesty International (not to mention Greenpeace, Friends of the Earth, the Pro-Life movement, etc.) Jo is married to Robert the man of her dreams, and they have ten lovely children: Andrew, Beth, Cather-

ine, David, Edward, Francis, George, Harry, Isobel and John. They all go to church together every Sunday and are deeply admired as a Model Christian Family.

Let's imagine this as a play. In Scene One we meet the family at Sunday lunch. Jo says grace and Robert carves the joint. Father Michael, their pastor, who has been invited to lunch, gazes around him and muses how God must love this wonderful Christian family.

In Scene Two, as in the original Job story, we move to the court of heaven where God is receiving his weekly report from the guardian angels. Rather to our surprise, Satan is there too, and God asks him what he's been up to. 'Oh, roaming about, here and there,' says Satan, not wanting to let on too much about his activities. 'Have you

seen my servant Joanna?' says God. 'Isn't she wonderful?' I'm so proud of her.'

'Humph!' says Satan. 'She's only good because she's scared of you. I'll bet you if things started to go wrong with her, she'd soon curse you to your face.' God is furious, but eventually agrees to let Satan test Jo, though he makes him promise not to touch a hair of her head.

In Scene Three we move back to Jo's house. At first it seems that the house is empty and then we see a figure huddled on the sofa sobbing. It is Jo. Her shoulders heave and she rocks to and fro moaning like an animal in pain. What on earth is wrong?

Then we hear the narrator's voice: the Evil one has acted swiftly and Jo's carefully ordered world has collapsed about her ears. Like a refugee, like an earthquake victim, she sits stunned and weeping amid the rubble. Then, in the sonorous tones of a wartime news-caster, the narrator reads out a list of the casualties: Robert, Jo's husband, has died suddenly of a coronary; Andrew, her first born, has died in an earthquake while on voluntary service in Mexico; Beth, the first of the twins, has been killed by terrorists in the Middle East while Catherine, devastated at the loss of her sister, has committed suicide; David, the ballet dancer, has died of AIDS in his London bedsit and Edward, who worked with Oxfam in Ethiopia, has died of starvation in solidarity with the famine victims; Francis, the wandering poet, who cared nothing for things material, has died of an overdose of heroin in Kathmandu and George, the soldier, has died in battle; Harry, the student, has been killed in a car crash, his sister Isobel raped and murdered; while John, the merry little boy with Down's syndrome, has died during surgery for the hole in his heart. Within a week, Jo has lost her entire family, as other women may lose those they love in time of war, famine or natural catastophe.

The narrator's voice fades away and we, the audience, sit completely aghast. At first there is silence, than a whisper and then a horrible keening sound, a howl of grief, like a wolf caught in a trap: 'Why, why me? What have I done to deserve this? How could God do this to me?'

The curtain falls and we file out woodenly for the intermission. Such grief is too much to handle, mind-blowing to the bystander, totally devastating to those personally involved. For our purposes, let us make this intermission a long one and explore not so much the answer to the question 'Why me?' as how one approaches the questioner. The pastoral care of the afflicted (and here I mean the sick, the bereaved and all whose lives have somehow been disrupted) must be tailored not only to the man or woman and his or her situation but to the *stage* of their personal journey. The *question* – Why me? – may be the same but the *response* will be different, depending upon whether it is the rhetorical wail of the recently bereft or the calculated angry question of someone struggling to make sense of his or her experience. When an individual is suddenly afflicted, finds that he or she has cancer or AIDS or multiple sclerosis, or is unexpectedly bereaved, that person frequently goes into a state of shock and disbelief. It is as though the mind cuts out from the pain of reality and retreats into a world of its own. A person in such a state may *ask* 'Why me?' but is in no state to process a carefully reasoned answer. Such questions are an expression of the individual's pain and need to be listened to rather than answered. More than anything, the person needs to be 'held', either metaphorically or actually, to be cocooned, and cherished until he is able to resume control of his life. This period of shock may last a few hours, days or even longer but the person will eventually emerge to experience the pain of loss.

1 PHASE of NUMBING
Shock – Numbness – Denial
Disbelief

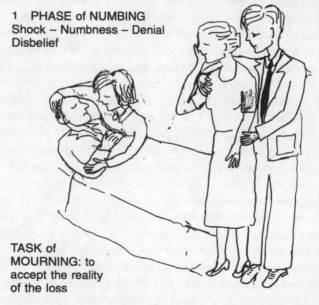

TASK of
MOURNING: to
accept the reality
of the loss

The second stage of mourning, the phase of acute grief, is characterized by an alternation between two states of mind: that of belief in the loss with consequent pangs of grief, pain and anger and a curious state of disbelief in which the person, unable to register the reality of his or her loss, searches for the missing person or object. Such searches, of course, are doomed to failure with a consequent sense of foolishness, frustration and renewed pain.

The emotions are very near the surface in acute grief and the bereaved experience a bewildering sequence of rage, anger, guilt and despair as they struggle to accept what is happening to them. Tears will come readily as will the 'pangs of grief', a sensation of sharp pain and despair which sweeps over people, engulfing them like a tidal wave and rendering them, for the moment, quite unable to function. Anger is a very common emotion in acute grief and it may be rational or quite irrational. It may be projected on to any available person, for example a relative or a professional carer or, in the case of a believer, it may be directed at God. It is in this situation that the question 'Why me?' may be articulated as: 'How could God do this to me? How can there be a God who allows this kind of suffering. It's not fair. If God is all-powerful, why doesn't he just abolish suffering?'

It is important to understand that although such questions have to be *asked*, they do not necessarily have to be *answered*. As in the earlier stage of mourning they are largely rhetorical questions, an expression of pain and grief, and much harm can be done by responding with pious platitudes when what is really needed is a listening ear and an acknowledgement of the awfulness of the situation. In most situations, the grief-stricken are asking the listener to *share* their grief, not to resolve it, because they know deep down, that is not possible. This stage of grieving, then, is not really the place for offering one's carefully reasoned and lovingly cherished beliefs about

2 PREOCCUPATION WITH IMAGES OF THE DECEASED

the meaning of suffering. If the person actually demands to know what we think or believe it is best to speak quietly and simply of one's faith in the loving providence of God rather than enter into an explanation which may well be misunderstood or rejected. In the long run, we must all remember, the question of suffering is a mystery and while theologians may write lengthy tomes and preach impassioned sermons, they do not really *know* the answer to the eternal questions.

It is, however, important that we be clear about one issue, and that is concerning anger with God. Because we are in awe of the majesty and power of God there is a natural tendency to feel that it is blasphemous to be angry with him; perhaps at a hidden level, too, we are afraid that, like Job, we might get an answer that we are not big enough to handle or that some divine ray gun will reduce us to a charred remnant. A closer glance at the Book of Job, however, should clarify the issues, for we find that not only does God prefer Job's fury to the mealy-mouthed obeisance of the Comforters, but that he does in fact listen to his complaint, even if God's answer is not quite what Job expects. There is, throughout the Old Testament, a long tradition of God's friends arguing with him. We see it in Moses as he protests his unsuitability for the mission imposed upon him, in Jacob as he wrestles with the angel and in the wretched Jeremiah as he complains that the Lord has been playing fast and loose with him:

> You have seduced me, Lord, and I have let myself be
>   seduced;
> you have overpowered me: you were the stronger.
> I am a daily laughing-stock,
>   everybody's butt. (Jer. 20:7)

Job, like Jeremiah, curses the day of his birth:

> May the day perish when I was born,
> and the night that told of a boy conceived. (Job 3:3)

It is important to understand, when dealing with the afflicted, that desperate men and women will often cry out in despair, 'Why did God let this happen to me? I wish I were dead!' when what they really mean is, 'It's not fair! I wish it would all go away. I can't cope with what's happening to me. Please help me.' They are like a bewildered, terrified child, kicking and screaming in its mother's arms. In the same way that a child must cry, so too must an adult express his pain and anger. We must beware of trying to step in between the grieving person and God, like an officious nanny saying self-rightouesly, 'Now, now, big boys don't cry. Mummy wouldn't like you to say things like that.' Instead, I believe, we should gently push the sufferer right into the arms of God, flailing fists, clenched teeth, snotty nose and all; the place for a desperate child is his parent's arms. It may well be, of course, that the grieving feel estranged, alienated from God and can find no comfort in prayer. All we can do then is 'hold' them, if they will let us, and encourage them to vent their fury, reminding them that God is big enough to take their anger and will answer them in his own time. The difficulty, of course, is that God's time is not necessarily our time.

After this digression let us return to our drama. The curtain rises on Act Two, Scene One, and we are back in Joanna's house. Some months have passed and Jo's wild grief has abated. We find her talking to her pastor and listen in amazement to the way she has coped with her tragedy. 'God has been very good to me,' she says with a gentle smile. 'I've had a wonderful loving husband and ten beautiful children. It God has chosen to take them from me, then that's his business. I can only trust him and try to rebuild my life.' Father Michael is silent in the face of a faith which he feels is a great deal stronger than his own. How on earth has this woman come to terms with such a tragedy in less than a year? Anyone else would have been completely destroyed, lost their faith, gone mad. (This is not a treatise on bereavement so I will resist the opportunity to explore the issue of whether or not Jo has come to terms with her loss or is somehow suppressing her grief, and move on to the next part of our story.)

In Act Two, Scene Two, we are back in the court of heaven, where God is once again deep in conversation with Satan. 'What did I tell you?' says God. 'You all but destroyed that poor girl's life and look, her faith is even stronger. *Now* are you satisfied?' Satan, of course is not satisfied, 'Ah,' he says, 'she's only lost her family. It's not as if she's had to suffer in her own body. I'll bet you if I really had a go at her it would be a different story.' God scowls. Clearly he feels trapped. If he continues his embargo on Jo's person, Satan will always be able to say, 'You haven't *really* tested her. If you lay a finger on her bone and flesh, I'll warrant you, she will curse you to your face.'

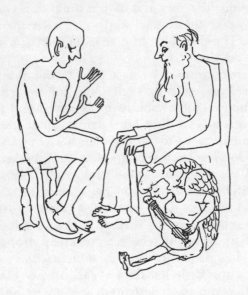

Eventually, God gives in and Satan goes off at speed to find Jo before God can change his mind. (If you find your hackles rising at this irreverent description of God, please go at once and read the Job story in your bible. Like the writer there, I am using this caricature for a very serious purpose.)

The curtain falls and rises again on Scene Three and of course, the worst has happened. Jo is in hospital, struck

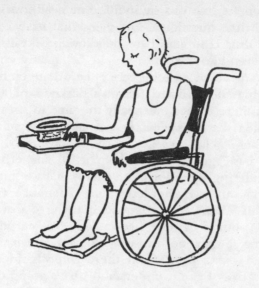

down by cancer. She is a pitiful sight, a bowed figure parked in a wheelchair in the radiotherapy department corridor. She has lost her hair as a result of chemotherapy and she clutches a vomit bowl desperately on her lap. The tears run unchecked down her pinched cheeks and like Job she mutters to herself: 'It's not fair. I'm so miserable. I feel so awful. Just look at me, bald as a coot with my bones all sticking out. Why is God doing this to me? He's poisoned by body, my soul, everything I ever loved. Whatever have I done to deserve this. How could God be so cruel?'

Poor Jo. What on earth can we say to her? Better perhaps to say nothing, and leave her in the hands of the kindly porter and the nurse who have mercifully appeared to take her back to the ward. My world is populated by the likes of Jo. Sometimes they get better and leave hospital to live happily ever after; more often, perhaps, they die, or linger on for months in indifferent health, asking the same terrible question: 'Why me? What have I done to deserve this? How can there be a loving God if he treats his children like this?'

While much of pastoral care is best done by listening, by sharing the afflicted person's darkness of rage and despair, there comes eventually the time to speak, to try to explain the inexplicable, to make sense of tragedy. What then? What are we to say? There are, I believe, certain basic guidelines to help us in answering these 'Why suffering' questions: the first is that we must speak only from our own knowledge and experience, from our own truth. We *all* feel inadequate in trying to answer these questions but if *we* have been asked, it is *our* ideas that are being sought, not those of the vicar down the road. This may mean that we sit there empty-handed saying weakly: 'Truly I don't understand what's going on, but I do believe that God is somehow here in the mess with you and that he loves you.' This may well be enough. If it isn't, and you don't know where to go from there, it's best to suggest the person speak to someone with some theological expertise. The second guideline is that, as always, we must temper our answer to the condition of the questioner. It is no earthly use my quoting great tracts of Job, however much they may help *me*, to someone to whom that kind of language is totally alien. Similarly, it's not a lot of use telling those who are plunged into despair and unbelief that Jesus died to save them and everything will be all right in heaven. As a Christian I actually believe precisely that: but as a pastoral carer I know that this kind of language is frequently unhelpful to those whose faith is under strain.

Let me assume, however, for our purposes that I am being questioned by someone who is *not* acutely grieving, who believes in God and in Christ but who is grappling,

as we all do, carers and sufferers alike, with the problem
of suffering. It is at this stage of our exploration that we
should go together to the original text of Job and listen
(for this is a very dramatic speech) to the opening words
of God as he addresses the wretched, complaining, Job.

'Who is this obscuring my designs
   with his empty-headed words?
Brace yourself like a fighter;

now it is my turn to ask questions and yours to inform me.
Where were you when I laid the earth's foundations?
Tell me, since you are so well informed!
Who decided the dimensions of it; do you know?
Or who stretched the measuring line across it?
What supports its pillars at their bases?
Who laid its corner stone
when all the stars of the morning were singing for joy,
and the Sons of God in chorus were chanting praise?'

On and on the questions come:

Who pent up the sea behind closed doors
when it leaped tumultuous out of the womb,
when I wrapped it in a robe of mist
and made black clouds its swaddling bands. . . ?

Have you ever in your life given orders to the morning
or sent the dawn to its post. . . ?
Have you journeyed all the way to the sources of the sea,
or walked where the Abyss is deepest?
Have you been shown the gates of Death
or met the janitors of Shadowland? (Job 38:2–17)

There is not space here to quote as much of the Lord's
answer to Job as I would like, but it is wondrously powerful
and beautiful and I urge you to read it, for it is in these
last chapters that the answers to our questions lie hidden.
I say 'hidden' because, while God's answer to Job is written
in a style and idiom accessible to the people of a particular
culture living over two thousand years ago, it is less readily
available to us. Let us return, therefore, to the imagery
of our own time, to where we began, with the lovely and
virtuous Joanna. We left her, you will recall, plunged once
more into darkness, this time with her own personal physi-

cal affliction. Like Job, she wails in distress and then, having summoned up all her strength, she demands an answer of God. 'What are you playing at, God?' she says. 'What have I done to deserve this? Haven't I always served you to the best of my ability? You took away my husband and my children, and I accepted it all as your will. And now you are doing this to me? What's going on. I've a right to know!'

And then, out of the whirlwind, perhaps in a dream, perhaps in the darkness of her despair in that hospital corridor, the answer comes – but it's not what Jo expects, just as it was not what Job expected:

> My little one, you just don't know what you are talking about. The earth is infinitely more mysterious and complicated than you can possibly understand.
>
> Where were you when I made the human body, fashioned it, bone and sinew, in its magnificent intricacy of form? Have you any idea of the delicate balance of your immune system? What happens in your cells when a piece of genetic material changes and a rogue cell takes off like a terrorist, planting onco-genes throughout your body like fire bombs in a department store? Has it ever occurred to you that such a delicately balanced organism will by its very nature break down from time to time? Don't you realise that you are part of the earth? What would happen to the planet if you and your family lived for ever? – you would end up huddled together like discarded plastic containers on an empty beach.

I could go on and on like the author of Job, but it would be no more comprehensible. The message of Job, as I understand it, is this: God's creation is as it is. It is infinitely wild and complex and we cannot hope to understand it all. Creation is also closely interdependent. Our human life is part of an interlocking system of nature and creatures, of a universe that is not static, but changing. It is of the very nature of our world that there is violence in it. The earth's crust is alive, it moves and volcanoes erupt. Animals prey upon each other – if they didn't the veldts and prairies would be full of old and sick and dying animals. People prey upon each other. Men and women are fragile, wounded creatures; they are insecure, suspicious, afraid of the unknown, afraid of losing what they have, and they guard their space and their possessions jealously. Human beings are alive as the earth and its creatures are alive; they have sexual desires, passions, lusts which they sometimes cannot control. They rape, pillage, murder, for survival, for gain, for fun. That is the world in which we live, the world made by our all-powerful creator God.

But it is also a world of incredible beauty, of mountains and sunsets, of glaciers and lush green valleys. It is the world of the seal, the dolphin and the polar bear, of the eagle, the humming bird and the territorial domestic robin. It is the world of poets and musicians, of ice skaters and ballet dancers, of scientists and geniuses of all kinds. It is a world of heroes as well as of cowards, of saints as well as sinners, of dedicated men and women who give their lives as a holocaust for those who cannot care for themselves. For every volcano erupting there are ten thousand quiet and fertile hillsides, for every rapist a hundred thousand lovers, whispering words of comfort, joy and ecstasy. This is the world that our God has made and, like the author of Genesis, I believe that it is very good.

So there you have your answer: 'Sorry Job, sorry Joanna, that's the way things are.' We can hardly say it's a very satisfactory answer, can we? And yet, it seems, Job *was* satisfied, for he says:

I know that you are all-powerful:
>   what you conceive, you can perform,
I am the man who obscured your designs
>   with my empty headed words,
I have been holding forth on matters I cannot
>   understand,
>   on marvels beyond me and my knowledge . . .
I knew you then only by hearsay;
>   but now, having seen you with my own eyes,
I retract all that I have said,
>   and in dust and ashes I repent. (Job 42:2–6)

The key to understanding Job's acceptance of God's answer lies in the penultimate two lines of this verse:

>   I knew you then only by hearsay;
>   but now I have seen you with my own eyes.

Job can accept God's answer because it has come directly from God in a mind-blowing personal encounter. Now that he has met God, Job realizes that his questions, although they seemed justified, were in fact irrelevant, *because his idea of God was all wrong.*

In the last chapters of the Book of Job, the carefully constructed stage set of the court of heaven with its God with a long white beard and Satan with his pitchfork are swept away. They disappear because they are only a fantasy, a projection, an invention of a people who have tried to fashion a god they can understand and control. The trouble is that we too are tempted to fashion idols, to project on to God all sorts of human qualities so that we can understand and therefore control him. But God is not like that. He is 'totally other'. He (She, It, They) has existed from all time, is beyond our world, beyond our understanding. This is what we mean when we say that God is *transcendent*, beyond all that we can understand.

This understanding of God is as old as humankind, as is the idea that God is like us. Men and women have always struggled to hold in tension the idea of the Divinity as utterly unknowable and mysterious and the idea of God as somehow accessible and concerned with our affairs. The primitive peoples resolved this tension by believing in a whole range of gods, one of whom was unknowable and the others who were accessible. Before the revelation of Sinai, the Israelites acknowledged El Shaddai, the god of the mountain, as the Creator, the controller of mysterious events like fertility and the seasons, but they had their domestic gods who travelled about with them, to whom they could tell their troubles and talk as a friend. The revelation at Sinai was a watershed event because it was the moment when God revealed that not only is he all-powerful, transcendent and beyond all knowing, but he is also *immanent*, that is close at hand, and that he loves his people with great passion. What God tried to teach his people in the first two commandments was that he was their only God and that they had no need of other gods: they should approach him directly. He described himself to Moses: 'Yahweh, Yahweh, a god of tenderness and compassion, slow to anger, rich in kindness and faithfulness.' (Exod. 34:6).

The Old Testament is full of such descriptions of God. In the first chapter of Deuteronomy the Lord reminds his people of the time when he carried them 'as a man carries his child', while in Hosea we read: 'I was like someone who holds an infant close against his cheek; stooping down to him I gave him his food' (1:3).

Again and again we hear this message: 'I, God, loved my people like a father.' But they did not understand – they could not grasp the concept that a mysterious all-powerful god was also good and loving. That is why the people of Israel made the golden calf: they just couldn't cope with the unseen god of Sinai; they had to have a god they could imagine and control. And we, of course are the same. We too find it hard to accept that God is as he is, and we make idols of him. Either he is a terrible dictator who doesn't care about us, or he is a loving daddy who would never hurt his children. When all goes well, we favour the second option, but when our world collapses, we say, like a frightened child, that daddy is wicked and cruel, and then we feel totally lost.

But there *is* another way. It *is* possible to integrate these two concepts of God, to learn that he is both transcendent and immanent, both beyond all knowing and as close to us as our mother's breast. It is the way of the scriptures, the way of the mystics and it is the way of Jesus of Nazareth, Emmanuel, God with us. Perhaps God realized that it was just too hard for most people to cope with his 'otherness' and that is why he sent his Son so that we could see with our own eyes what God was like. But even in Jesus' own day it was hard, and Jesus was exasperated when one of the disciples asked, 'Lord, let us see the Father and then we shall be satisfied!'

'Philip!' Jesus said, 'Have I been with you all this time, and still you do not know me. . . Do you not believe that I am in the Father and the Father is in me?' (John 14:8).

Finally, let us try to integrate the Judaeo-Christian understanding of the mystery of suffering that is our spiritual heritage and should be our support and our comfort. The message goes like this: God, who is all-powerful and infinitely mysterious, made the world. He made it in his own way, intricate and beautiful, wild and dangerous. He filled it full of plants and living creatures, the most complex and self-aware of whom was man. God appointed men and women as *stewards* of the earth, to live on it, to cherish it but not to plunder and detroy it. It is in the nature of this world, of all God's creatures, that they are frail and vulnerable and that they die. Nothing and no one lives for ever. All matter is eventually recycled, as people, as animals, as stardust. That is the way things are. On this earth we are all sojourners, because we are all destined ultimately to return to the Divine, to the heart of God from whence we come.

If we were angels, of course, we would understand the truth that death is not a tragedy, that it is quite simply the beginning of the life for which we were originally created. But then we are not angels, we are creatures and we see, as Paul put it, 'through a glass darkly.' How then can we not be sad when we or those we love are afflicted or face death? This is what it means to be human: to be frail and vulnerable in our bodies, to be storm-tossed in our emotions, to be limited in our understanding. We forget, however, that this is the way the One Holy Transcendent God made people and that, when he had finished, he smiled upon his work and declared that it was very, very good.

2

Work in the Dark Valley

'Though I walk in the valley of the shadow of death, no evil will I fear.' (Psalm 23)

I WORK WITH PEOPLE who are in hell. That is my calling. I bring them what comfort I can, water to soothe parched lips, a salve for blistered wounds, opium to relieve pain, but I cannot free them. My pass through the locked gates is in my name only. I can come and go at will, but no one may leave with me. That, I suppose, is *my* greatest pain: I long to make a break for it, carrying these frail and wounded victims on my back until we are safely across the river, out of reach of the guards. But that, alas, cannot be. Mine is simply the role of prison visitor, of comforter, of companion: I do not hold the keys. The liberator will come in his own good time, not in theirs, nor yet in mine. So we wait together, my people and I, ears straining for the sound of his voice, for that longed for cry, 'Awake O sleeper, and arise from the dead . . .'

Working with the dying is a messy business, both physically and emotionally. People vomit or need the commode just when one is discussing some vital spiritual issue. They get fed up or tired after a very few minutes, and make it clear that they've had enough. It takes quite a while, then, to tune in to this sort of work, to give counsel when it's

[25]

asked for – and be silent when it's not. It takes time, too, to learn to be content with just a few sentences, to relax and be a hollow instrument in God's hands so that the words and the music are his, not ours.

Before I go any further, or let my delight in imagery run away with me, let me explain the background from which I write and put my credentials, or lack of them, clearly on the table. I write as a hospice doctor, a cradle Roman Catholic, who for the past twelve years has worked with men and women dying of cancer. I have had no training in pastoral counselling, but I have attended many deathbeds and walked alongside men and women of every age, faith and condition, as they have moved fearfully or peacefully towards their death.

My other qualification, if I dare to call it that, is that I 'keep company' with God. By this I mean that, not only do I pray, day in, day out, with greater or lesser fidelity, but that my mind and heart return to God off and on during the day rather in the way that the needle of a compass returns automatically to due north. This adventure of prayer has given me an understanding of certain truths which I suspect cannot be acquired simply by the study of theology.

CREDO

I believe in God:
One
Holy
Transcendent
beyond all knowing.
I believe he created the Universe,
the sun, the moon, the stars
all living things.

Work in the Dark Valley

I believe he holds the whole world
in his hands, safely, now.

I believe that God is good,
that he is loving,
that he is truth,
that he is freedom.

I believe God knows
both my lying down and my rising,
my depression and my laughter.

I believe God loves me,
for richer, for poorer,
in sickness and in health,
in triumph or in failure,
in virtue or in sin,
until we meet
in death.

I believe, don't ask me how,
that I know God.

Not through my eyes
nor through my seeing,
not through my ears
nor through my hearing,
not through my hands
nor through my touching,
but deep, deep in my heart,
I know the unknowable God
through Christ, his only son.

From this very personal, this almost carnal knowledge
of God, I have deduced other things:

I believe that God loves people,
all people.
Not just the good, the pure,
the beautiful,
the Christians,
but EVERYONE.

I believe he loves
the mad, the bad,
the mean, the greedy
dictators, child abusers,
terrorists, murderers,
EVERYONE.

God is not mocked, he is not blind.
He reads the hearts twisted by hate,
the minds clouded by cupidity.
He sees shining
the grains of truth, invisible to men,
the seeds of goodness, lying dormant,
awaiting a rain,
a sun that sometimes fails.

This, then, is the faith which I bring to my people. This
is the light by which I walk, the strength which makes it
possible for me to live my life 'on the margins of the
bearable'. But how, you may reasonably ask, does it work
in practice? What do I say? How do I get over to people
that God loves them?

The answer, of course, is complex. There is no simple
formula for pastoral care, nor can one single person do
it all. Dying people are both needy and vulnerable, human
beings stripped of their protection, naked and embar-
rassed like a snail without its shell or a moulting bird.
They are physically weak, unpleasing to the eye, men and

women of sorrows, acquainted with grief. Frequently, they are disfigured, hard to look upon, people to make us screen our faces, all too easily despised and rejected by their fellows.

What such people need, therefore, and what we must provide, is a place of refuge, a space both physical and emotional where they can feel safe, accepted just as they are. To be accepted, however, is only the beginning, for beyond acceptance we all need to be valued, to know that we have worth, to be loved.

If I were to sum up our pastoral care in the hospice, I would say that we *reveal to people that they are lovable*. We do that both as an organization, as a community of carers, and as individuals in a one-to-one relationship with each suffering person. This means, in practice, that we take infinite care in providing friendly surroundings, comfortable beds and good food. More important by far, however, is the way we relate to people. It is a constant source of wonder to me to see and hear the nurses talking to the patients and their relatives. There is a totally unconscious courtesy and tenderness which leaves people in no doubt as to their value. The patients arrive, soiled and dishevelled, with their digestion awry and their hair unkempt. Almost without them realizing it, their dignity is restored and they are able to relax and let go of at least some of their pain.

This background music of loving and acceptance is, of course, only the beginning of pastoral care. More important than the acceptance of people's physical deformity is the unequivocal acceptance of their shadow side, of their anger, their meanness and their sin.

The American psychotherapist Carl Rogers has described the conditions for growth in a therapeutic relationship, be it between therapist and client, pastor and penitent, or teacher and student. Rogers speaks of 'congruence', by which he means that the therapist (doctor, pastor, parent) should be aware of his own feelings and act out of them, that he should not put on a façade, act out a role, or a pretence. Doctors and clergy perhaps more than anyone can fall into this trap of pretence. Because we feel inadequate, insecure in the face of another's pain, we fear that people will not trust us and we therefore put on a sort of emotional white coat or dog-collar in the hope that our persona will inspire the other with confidence. The tragedy is, of course, that role playing of this kind has exactly the opposite effect. The more we pretend to be something we're not, the more people pick up our falsity and the more they become insecure and afraid. Conversely, once we have the courage to be ourselves, however inadequate and foolish, the people we are with feel safe and we find, to our amazement, that we have the power to heal.

The secret is, I believe, that there is something enormously healing in being accepted. If I can go to my psychotherapist, weep into my coffee, give vent to my anger and admit that I hate X or Y, then I am already opening myself up to the power of healing. It is in this context that Rogers talks of UPR, 'unconditional positive regard'. By this he means the attitude in the therapist which conveys the message: 'I will accept you whatever you bring to me. There is nothing that you can say which will make me reject you.' Come to me, all you who are burdened and I will give you rest.

UPR, it seems to me, is *the* divine attribute. 'Be not afraid,' Jesus is always saying, 'Come to me, all you who are thirsty. Come to me, sinners and tax collectors, fallen women and perverts, child abusers and lost sheep, and I will make you whole.' When we welcome the sinner, then, we are doing God's work, forgiving seventy times seven, being a hollow conduit for his healing grace.

The wonderful thing about the grace of God is, of course, that it is like the Spirit herself: it is no respecter of persons or of theological boundaries. Although I as a Catholic value the sacrament of reconciliation and find it a powerful visible sign of God's invisible grace, I do not for one moment think that God's grace can be confined. The grace of God is like our child's conception of a ray gun – it is invisible, all-penetrating, defies all barriers. When I speak in this manner I am in no way denying my Christian heritage, merely acknowledging the greatness and inscrutability of the Divine.

I've no idea if this is orthodox theology, nor do I particularly care, for I speak of what I see, of what I experience day by day. I have learned long since that Christians have no monopoly on goodness, that unbelievers are as capable of heroic generosity as anyone, in short, that the Spirit listeth where it will. It follows, I believe, from this, that traditional sacramental care is only a small part of pastoral care – perhaps the least important part. I do not deny that religious people need religious rituals, nor that I personally shall want the sacraments when I am dying. But I know too that by far the most important sacrament of God's love is the tenderness, compassion and unconditional loving of carers. I know few things holier than the sight of an eighteen-year-old auxiliary nurse holding the hand and smoothing the withered cheek of an old man who is dying.

> The angels keep their ancient places;
>> Turn but a stone and start a wing!
> 'Tis ye, 'tis your estranged faces
>> That miss the many-splendoured thing. . . .
>
> Yea, in the night, my soul, my daughter,
>> Cry, clinging heaven by the hems,

[31]

And lo, Christ walking on the waters,
Not of Gennesareth, but Thames!*

Whilst I believe that this Christ-like attitude of unconditional acceptance and loving is the single most important element in the pastoral care of dying people, there
are other more specific tasks to be attempted in order to
assist an individual to find spiritual peace. Central to this
task is understanding the nature of the person's 'God
concept'. Many of the Christians I care for believe in a
loving father God and have no great fears of meeting him
(or her). There are a few people, however, who see God
as a harsh judge and are terrified of facing judgement. I
remember clearly one elderly lady who was quite sure that
God did not love her. When I asked her why, she said,
'I've been so wicked.' I asked her very gently what she
had done and she told me that, when a very beautiful
young woman in her twenties, she had seduced the husbands of two of her best friends! I arranged for her to
see a priest, and the next day she died, at peace with God
and man.

While it would ordinarily be intrusive for a medical
carer to ask a patient to speak of their sins, it is, I believe,
fundamental to good pastoral care to 'screen' actively for
fear of God, guilt and unresolved conflict. This screening
need not be too 'heavy' a business. I would ask people if
they are afraid, if there is anything worrying them, if there
is anything they'd like to ask. I would normally ask people
directly about their faith: 'Do you have any sort of faith
in God, or in an afterlife?' If people say no, I would leave
it at that. If they say yes, I would ask if they pray, and try
to get a feel for the kind of God they believe in. It would
always be my aim to mobilize whatever spiritual resources

* Francis Thompson, from 'The Kingdom of God'.

a person has available to them, in order to give them as much strength and comfort as possible for the painful weeks ahead.

Underpinning each carer's concept of what needs to be done for people facing death is the ministering person's own theology, their understanding of God, of the relationship of the Creator with his/her creatures. The carer who believes that only baptized Christians can be 'saved' will clearly be more anxious to achieve a deathbed conversion than someone who is utterly confident in the unfathomable mercy of God. In writing about pastoral care, I can speak only of my own experience and how I have grown in my understanding of what Catholics call the Four Last Things: Death, Judgement, Heaven and Hell.

When I was a theologically naïve medical student, fairly fresh from convent school, I believed that unbaptized babies could not go to heaven. Moved by this belief, I solemny (though clandestinely) baptized aborted foetuses in the operating theatre. I remember so well standing at the sink slowly running the tap on to those tiny misshapen bodies lying in a kidney dish and saying to myself, 'I baptize you in the name of the Father, Son and Holy Ghost!' Did I really believe in a God who would consign innocent babies to limbo? I suppose I did – though it seems a very long time ago.

If I don't believe in limbo now, what *do* I believe? What about heaven and hell? Where do these time-honoured concepts fit into the spiritual care of dying people? Is pastoral care really about preparing people to meet their Maker, getting them to repent of their sins and accept Jesus as their Lord and Saviour? I'm sorry, but I don't believe it is. The Jesus I meet in the gospels, Yahweh, the compassionate and rich in mercy, the transcendent God whom I meet in the darkness of my unknowing prayer, speaks to me not of judgement and perdition but of mercy and love.

A couple of years ago, while I was at mass in a Poor Clare convent in Florida, my mind dwelt with great pain upon the predicament of a friend, a Catholic priest who was dying of AIDS. So certain was he that his community would reject him that he had told no one and relied for support on his hospital carers and friends. As I knelt there I worried about his immortal soul, wondering if he was estranged, not only from his brethren in religion, but from the God to whom he had pledged lifelong fidelity. My musing was interrupted by the final hymn and as I stood there listening, my heart swelled:

> There's a wideness in God's mercy
>   Which is wider than the sea.
> There's a kindness in his judgement
> Which is more than liberty.
> For the love of God is broader
> Than the measure of man's mind,
> And the heart of the Eternal
>   Is most wonderfully kind.

As I heard that hymn I *knew* that my 'David' was all right, that we, his friends, must support him in his bodily and emotional frailty until he fell into the outstretched arms of God.

That, then, is my theology: I 'know' deep in my guts that the heart of the Eternal God is most wonderfully kind and that his mercy is infinitely wider than the grey sea which swells before me as I write. I believe that when we die we are born ino eternal life with God – and that life is what we call heaven. If my patients ask me what *I* believe I tell them. I tell them that I believe that when we die, not only are we with God but that we are somehow more alive, more vibrant, more ourselves than we have ever been before. Just how this is I do not know – but if life with God is for real, then surely it's about a fullness of life which is unimaginably wonderful.

How I actually say this will depend, of course, upon the person to whom I am speaking, for language must always be tempered to the other's culture and understanding. This kind of work is highly intuitive and I usually don't know what I'm going to say until I've said it. I remember vividly one such conversation. Joy was a young woman in her thirties dying of a cancer which had spread to her lungs. One day I went to see her just as her priest was leaving. 'I've just been planning my funeral,' she said gloomily. If ever there was a conversation stopper, that must surely be it! Not knowing what to say for the best, I crossed my fingers and spoke from my heart. 'It's got to be a party, Joy,' I said, 'It's got to be a rave-up! This is the beginning, not the end!' She grinned and squeezed my hand. 'You give me *so* much strength', she said, 'when you talk like that.'

Clearly that kind of pastoral care cannot be planned in advance; it can only flow out of one's own spiritual well which, in its turn, must be constantly refilled from the source.

Although I have a rather old-fashioned and perhaps childlike belief in heaven, I do not, on the other hand, believe in eternal damnation, i.e. I do not believe in hell. Let me try to unpack that last bold statement, for I suspect I am going against centuries of tradition of my own and other churches. I find the Dantesque notion of hell as a place of eternal fire and punishment simply incompatible with the idea of a loving God. Perhaps my problem is akin to that of the people who find they can't believe in God because they cannot reconcile the notion of a loving Creator with the existence of suffering. Perversely, I have no problem with God and the suffering of the world: I just accept that they both *are*, and I am quite content to leave the mystery of it to God and get on with trying to patch up his wounded people. I believe, moreover, that God is somehow *in* the suffering of the world:

I believe that God
has the whole world in his hands.
He is not a bystander
at the pain of the world.

He does not stand like Peter
wringing his hands in the shadows
but is there, in the dock, on the rack,
high on the gallows tree.
He is in the pain of the lunatic, the tortured,
those racked by grief.
His is the blood that flows in the gutter,
His are the veins burned by heroin,
His the lungs choked by AIDS.
His is the heart broken by suffering,
His the despair
of the mute, the oppressed,
the man with a gun to his head.

He is the God of Paradox,
the God of Power
made impotent,
the God of Love.

I know that there are those who will take me to task for what they see as a soft and spurious theology which completely ignores the justice of God. I can understand that viewpoint for I am only too painfully aware of cruelty and evil in the world. I know too that there are those with whom I would not wish to share my particular corner of heaven: the abuser of children, the muggers of old ladies, the rapists, the torturers and the cruel, greedy, uncaring manipulators of power.

Much as I dislike these people, however, I cannot believe in their eternal damnation: the mercy of the God whom I know is simply too big. So what then? How can I explain that away?

The answer, I believe, lies in the notion of our common woundedness. I believe that by the very virtue of being human we are, to a greater or lesser degree, flawed. I, for example, have certain frailties which are the direct result of the genes I carry, the effect of my childhood nurture and the things that have happened to me over the years. It is clearly no fault of mine that I was born two years before the war, that my mother sent me away to save me from the Blitz, and that as a result of this *perceived* rejection I am forever emotionally needy, demanding, insecure. My mother, of course, should have known better, but then she was the child of a cool and rather formal marriage, of a young woman who was herself emotionally needy. And so it goes on. The 'sins', the frailties of the parents are indeed 'visited' upon the children, unto the third and the fourth generation.

I am lucky that all that happened to me was that I thought myself unloved and therefore unlovable. Had I been physically abused I might have grown into a physical abuser, like thousands of unhappy people. The more I understand my own frailties and those of others, the more I see that we are only partially culpable.

If I have little belief in individual human wickedness, however, I have a deep sense of the power of evil in the world. It's not that I believe in personified evil, in the devil, but I am conscious of evil as a force to be reckoned with. Like Paul, I can complain that the good which I would like to do escapes my anxious grasp, while I always seem to be doing that of which I am ashamed. I am arrogant and insensitive, greedy, manipulative, just as other people are – it is part of my fallen humanity.

These, of course, are relatively minor frailties. What, then, is the origin of *real* evil, of the demon which possesses a group of ordinary human beings and turns them into a cruel, destructive mob? We have seen this so recently in the riots in our own cities and in Germany, where ordinary folk get worked up to fever pitch and kill a policeman, burn people's houses or turn on a group of terrified refugees. But even here one can try to understand something of what is happening. I, who am intelligent and creative and have well-paid work which I enjoy, can only begin to imagine the grey desolation of bored unemployed youngsters with nothing to do all day long but hang listlessly around street corners waiting for something to happen. Evil as mob violence is, there is something worse: the cold-blooded, calculated wickedness of those who use their power to oppress others, those who manipulate their fellows for personal gain. What happens to the crooked financiers of this world, to the drug barons, to the 'godfathers' of the Mafia? I do not know. I cannot imagine. Perhaps these are the 'self-damned' who cut themselves off from the love of God. But even these sad people can be changed by the power of God:

> I believe that pain and prayer,
>   are somehow saved, processed, stored,
> used in the Divine Economy.
> The blood shed in Salvador
> will irrigate the heart of some financier
> a million miles away.
> The terror, pain, despair,

swamped by lava, flood or earthquake
will be caught up like mist
and fall again, a gentle rain
on arid hearts or souls despairing
in the back streets of Brooklyn.

Although I find myself unable to believe in Dante's inferno, in the fires of Gehenna which will never go out, I am more at home with Irenaeus' concept of hell as the formless part of creation which has never been worked on by God. For second-century Irenaeus, hell was akin to the primordial chaos of Genesis, the formless void over which the spirit brooded. It has echoes for me of the Greek underworld or Hades, the desolate and uncultivated shores of the infernal regions where the soil was barren and no living thing could survive, for the sun's rays could not penetrate there. It was the land of black polars, of the willows which never bore fruit. Long before the Greeks described Hades, the Sumerian legends spoke of the *apsu*, the abyss under the earth to which men descended after death. It was known as the Land of No Return and was guarded by seven walls. As a man entered successively through these gates he was stripped of all his garments until he found himself naked and imprisoned for ever in the 'dwelling place of the shadows'.

I find this description chillingly familiar, with its echoes of Auschwitz or the relentless progress of Alzheimer's disease, cancer or AIDS. That is why I said at the beginning of this article that I work with those who are in hell.

I think as I write of one of my patients who died this very day. His grief as he faced death was terrible to share, for he saw nothing but his own failing strength and the fact that he would soon be parted from his wife. Now, Sandy is dead and his wife must begin the long bereavement journey, without him.

But what of Sandy, where is he? Is it all over as his corpse lies in the undertaker's fridge? I do not think so. Like Irenaeus I believe that 'Jesus descended into the lower part of the earth, the unworked, formless part of creation, in order to see it with his own eyes and to make it his own.' He went to forge meaning out of what was meaningless, out of death.

It is in this ancient tradition of Christ's harrowing of hell that I take comfort. Having once seen the amazing fresco of the Anastasis in the church of the Chora in Istanbul, I can never again despair. In this twelfth century painting of a much older tradition, Christ strides purposefully into hell and, taking Adam and Eve firmly by the wrists, pulls them unceremoniously out of the darkness into his own wonderful light.

But how could I explain this to Sandy? I couldn't. All I could do was to be present to him, to hold his hand, to hug him, to give him the drugs which suppressed the memories of his mother screaming in the Blitz. I could tell him gently that I believed that he and his wife would meet again – I could act out of my faith, but I couldn't give it to him. In the end, I think that doesn't matter. Perhaps it was part of Sandy's purification that he endure the ignominy of his failing body and the tricks of his troubled mind. What matters now is that he has exchanged the gentle touch of my hand upon his wrist for the powerful clasp of the unseen God.

3

Good Friday:
the Loneliness of the Virgin

ON GOOD FRIDAY we come together as a group of Christian people to keep vigil and to remember an event that happened in the Middle East nearly two thousand years ago. We remember that a Galilean carpenter, who believed himself to be the Son of God, was arrested and condemned to death and executed because he was somehow a threat to the established church and to the security of the state. There are a lot of people who think that Jesus of Nazareth was a deluded fool, that his death was an unfortunate result of petty local politics, and there are an awful lot more who just are not interested in the story at all.

But we – what do we believe? What bearing has our faith upon our own lives, let alone upon the lives of the people amongst whom we live? Those of us who share the faith of that Galilean carpenter believe that he was indeed the Son of God, and that his violent and terrible death is somehow the most important thing that has happened in the whole history of humankind.

As far as I can work out, the practice of spending three hours in vigil on Good Friday began in Latin America, in Peru, in the seventeenth century, with the Jesuit Fathers. The celebration was called 'La Soledad de la Virgen' (The

Loneliness of the Virgin), and it is still celebrated today all over Latin America.

Here I will try as best I can to draw some meaning out of the terrible events we commemorate on Good Friday. And to begin I would like to look at the passion of Christ through the eyes and heart of his mother, because perhaps no one sees or feels a man's pain as clearly or acutely as his mother.

I should explain to you now that this exploration is new to me, for, unlike many Catholics, I have had no devotion at all to the blessed virgin. I suspect I have been put off by a lot of very sentimental devotion and some very bad paintings and statues of an over-pious young woman in a pale-blue veil. The church in which all Christians have their roots, however, holds Mary in very high esteem, so it seems time to lay my prejudices on one side and try to hear what the theologians were saying. The story begins in St Luke's Gospel, when a teenage girl had a vision of an angel who told her that she had found favour with God and that she was to bear his son. St Luke doesn't tell us how Mary felt – but we can imagine. She must have been amazed, terrified, filled with awe, overwhelmed. Here was she, a woman without a husband, chosen by God to bear his son – to be fruitful in a way that no other human being had been before. I wonder, would she have thought of Sarah, the mother of Isaac, a barren woman made fertile by the power of God? If she hadn't been so frightened she might have laughed, like Sarah, and said 'You must be joking, no one has babies without a husband.' But she didn't – she just said, 'Yes, I'm yours, Lord, do what you want with me.'

It is this acceptance of Mary's, her *fiat* to God's request, that makes her important for us. It is her giving up of her own plans and total acceptance of the divine will that makes her a model for all Christians in their relationships with God. In this, Mary is like Abraham in the rather terrifying story of the sacrifice of Isaac. It's difficult for us, from such a different culture, to feel comfortable with Abraham's unquestioning obedience to such a terrible command – and yet we know that sometimes God seems to ask terrible sacrifices of his people, and if they say Yes he uses them in an amazing way.

Right from the beginning, then, Mary knew that this child of hers was different, that he had a destiny far beyond her comprehension. We hear her in the Magnificat, the words Luke gives her when she goes to visit her cousin Elizabeth, the mother of John the Baptist. 'The Almighty has done great things for me, Holy is his name.'

Perhaps when the baby was born she was lulled into a false sense of security – after all, he was weak and vulnerable, just like any other baby. But then, when she went to present him to the priest in the temple, there was Simeon's terrifying prophesy: 'You see this child: he is destined for the fall and for the rising of many in Israel, destined to be a sign that is rejected – and a sword will pierce your own soul too, so that the secret thoughts of many may be laid bare' (Luke 2:34–5).

This image of Mary with her soul pierced by a sword used to be a very popular one when I was a child, and there were lots of gruesome devotional pictures to depict it. Such pictures, which used to be so helpful to previous generations, put me off so completely that I discarded Mary as a sentimental figure who had no place in my own devotional world.

But the real Mary was flesh and blood, a woman whose suffering had probably lined her face and made her eyes dark with pain. I find the Mary I see in the Russian icons much easier to accept than the pale blonde girl demurely holding a lily. The Russian Orthodox have a great devotion to Mary dating from the very early days of the Eastern Church.

It was the second-century theologian Origen who named Mary as the 'Mother of all the Faithful', basing his thoughts on the passage in St John's Gospel when, as John and Mary stand at the foot of the cross, Jesus says to them, 'Son behold thy mother, and Mother behold thy son' (John 19:26). St John here stands as an archetype, a representative of all God's people, and Christ gives him Mary as his mother.

At the Council of Nicea in the fifth century, Mary was given the title of 'Mother of God', from which we get the lovely Orthodox word 'Theotokos', or God-bearer.

So Mary, by her *fiat*, by her unconditional acceptance of God's will, bore him into the world, in the same way that we, if we make the same *fiat* to whatever he asks of us, will carry him like a light in the darkness.

But this carrying of God is a costly business. Let us walk with Mary, as she follows her son to Golgotha. A nineteenth-century Russian poet, Aleksej Remizov, captures better than I can the grief of that journey. He begins this part of his story in heaven, when the Lord tries to send an angel to tell Mary that her son has been arrested. First he asks Gabriel, then Michael, then Raphael, but one by one they refuse, each appalled at the task of causing such pain to the spotless one.

In fear and trembling, their blazing white wings crossed the one over the other,
tears flowing from their burning bright eyes,
they refuse. . . .

The poet tells us that a little bird, a tiny linnet, heard the lamenting in heaven and flew down to earth, perching on the windowsill of the Mother of God.

Nodding his head like a sunflower,
    he began to sing
    a sad, sad song.

Mary looked up and found herself looking into the
wild, dark, hopeless eyes of Judas Iscariot, the disciple
who had betrayed his master.

The Mother of God arose
        but fell back again upon the window-seat –
        the linnet sang sadly,
    woeful, little bird.
Anguish enveloped her, and pierced to the heart
    by a horrifying presentiment, the Mother of God
        ran to the door.
'O Mary, where is your Son?'
John the apostle stopped her on the doorstep:
'O Mary, where is our Lord, our Master?'
And in the street, along the road,
        beneath her windows they were leading
        Christ:
and he was freely going to death on a cross.

Think what it must have been like for Mary at that
moment. What is it like for any mother when the police
come to take away her son? What is it like when she hears
a crash and comes out to see what has happened and
realizes that the child under the lorry is her child. How
truly Simeon spoke when he said, 'A sword shall pierce
your heart'.

Who will comfort a mother who has lost her son?
Who will give her refuge?
Who will shelter her in the dark night of grief?
To whom can she turn?

– the linnet, terrified by the shouting, flies away;
– the lips of the beloved disciple are sealed by grief.
Who will console her?
She is alone, the Mother of God.
She is forsaken – trodden down like grass –
She falls to the ground,
  (motionless, like a corpse) but again she rose up.
A groaning pierced her heart through and through.
Her hair was in disarray;
 (her head was spinning) her sight was blurred;
She ran headlong down the street
  and she saw the Son.
A heavy cross weighed down his shoulders.
His knees sagged under the blows;
  and at every step he bent nearer and nearer to the
   ground.
With her head unveiled, overcome by woe,
 and stumbling,
the Mother of God followed behind Christ.*

I love this portrait of Mary because it is so real. Here is
a woman distraught and dishevelled, wild with grief. Here
indeed we have the loneliness of the virgin, the mother
of God who has been named our mother as well. Surely
this Mary stands as an archetype of all the grieving
mothers of the world. She is the mother of the toddler
killed on Merseyside, of the Bosnian children suffocated
to death in the rescue lorry, of all the women of El Salvador, Argentina or Chile whose sons have been killed by
the military.

What then are we to do with this image, with this grief-
struck woman? To what purpose are we exposing ourselves

* Aleksej Remizov, from Theotokos 1989 Icon Book Calendar,
St Paul Media Productions.

to such grief, such pain? Of what use are we as impotent bystanders, standing useless beside the cross? There is a sense, of course, in which we *are* useless. We cannot bring back the dead and we cannot take away the grief of the bereaved. We have two choices – to admit our powerlessness and run away – or to admit our powerlessness and *stay*, impotent, in solidarity with the dying and the bereaved. I find this is very often my own calling. Although I can relieve the pain of my dying patients, I cannot halt the dying process. All I can do is accompany them in their grief and their anger – *be there* for them, share their darkness and their fear. I have learned, over many years, that there is a great power in this seemingly useless work. Those enduring great distress know that the cup cannot be taken away from them, but they value the presence of someone to share, however minimally, in their suffering – someone to 'watch' with them during their agony. Jesus himself, when wrestling with his fear in the Garden of Olives, begged his disciples to stay with him: 'Could you not watch one hour with me?'

So, perhaps today is a preparation, a practice for watching with Christ as he comes to us in our own lives. It is a practice for sitting up all night drinking endless cups of tea and listening to the desperate talk of the woman whose husband has walked out on her or who has dropped dead on the golf course. Waiting is never easy. It is tiring and tedious and one longs for release. But the dying have no release. Jesus has no release, and he calls us to watch with him.

4

Good Friday:
the Emptiness of God

CHRIST HANGS upon the cross. He is not a pretty sight.

When they nailed him to the cross, from his wounds
    blood flowed down and soaked the earth.
Inconsolable, the Mother of God stood at the foot
    of the cross, and at her side was John, the beloved
        disciple.
She could see every moment of his torment
    – and she could do nothing to ease it.
He asked for a drink – her heart was breaking –
    and she could not give him a drink
    (she dare not move from the foot of the cross).
And the sky grew dark:
    the swirling clouds thickened turbulent, menacing,
    the clouds grew dense, darkness grew deeper
and the clouds drove storms to the ends of the earth.
Over the city they loomed ominously
    and from their fiery depths flames shot to earth.
The appearance of Christ altered:
    his face grew pale; his hair hung limp.
'O God, my God, why did you bring me into being?;
    And his head dropped down upon his breast.

At the other side of Jerusalem, in the garden of
    Magdalene,
bowed down towards the ground, hanging by his leather
    belt,
the disciple who betrayed the Master – Judas:
    eyes unseeing in despair, wild eyes, in black hollow-
        looking sockets,
    were fixed on the stricken earth and his mouth was
        full of dust. (A. Remizov)*

I find this juxtaposition of the deaths of Jesus and Judas,
his betrayer, very powerful, for it highlights the whole
purpose of Christ's sacrifice: that he died for sinners, for
all the petty, greedy, cruel men and women who ever had
and ever would live upon this earth. What a waste it seems,
what an unfair exchange. *We* wouldn't agree to such a
transaction today. We wouldn't trade the life of one good
man for any number of terrorists, murderers, rapists, child
abusers. But then we are not God. His ways are not our
ways. How long it takes us to learn that! I find that I have
to try again and again to understand it – and still I forget
and get misled into imagining an all-powerful God, sitting
in splendour on a throne or making a triumphal entry
into Jerusalem. It's hardly surprising, then, that the Jews
got it wrong. For generations they had awaited the messiah, longing for the moment of their deliverance. I
wonder, had they confused the scriptural passages describ-
ing the glory of God with the kind of messiah God would
send to save them? When Isaiah received his call to be a
prophet he had an amazing vision of God, with the Lord
seated high on a throne, his train filling the sanctuary,
guarded by two angels.

No wonder the Jews thought that the Messiah would

* From *Theotokos*, 1989 Icon Book Calendar.

come in glory – but that wasn't part of God's plan. The more I think about it, the more mind-boggling I find the revelation of God which occurs during Christ's passion. Here we have the fulfilment of another vision of Isaiah, that of the suffering servant of Yahweh:

See, my servant will prosper,
he shall be lifted up, exalted, rise to great heights.

As the crowds were appalled on seeing him
– so disfigured did he look
that he seemed no longer human –
so will the crowds be astonished at him,
and kings stand speechless before him;
for they shall see something never told
and witness something never heard before:
'Who could believe what we have heard,
and to whom has the power of Yahweh been revealed?'
Like a sapling he grew up in front of us,
like a root in arid ground.
Without beauty, without majesty (we saw him),
no looks to attract our eyes;
a thing despised and rejected by men,
a man of sorrows and familiar with suffering,
a man to make people screen their faces:
he was despised and we took no account of him. (Isa.
    52:13–53:3)

It is in this broken figure, this man of sorrows, that we are asked to look for the Messiah. How difficult it is to believe that this was how it was meant to be. It's much easier to imagine that somehow Jesus' plans had gone wrong – that he'd spoken out once too often and been 'removed', as revolutionaries and prophets are always being 'removed' for the security of the state. But, if we look closely at what Jesus said during his ministry, and especially during the last weeks and days of his life, we find that somehow he had always known that this messy, ignominious death was part of God's plan for him. We see this very clearly when Jesus, after his triumphal entry into Jerusalem, said:

> 'Now the hour has come
>   for the Son of Man to be glorified.
> I tell you, most solemnly,
> unless a wheat grain falls on the ground and dies,
> it remains only a single grain;
> but if it dies,
> it yields a rich harvest.
> Anyone who loves his life loses it;
> anyone who hates his life in this world
>   will keep it for the eternal life.' (John 12:23–5)

But it wasn't just asceticism that Jesus was preaching, it was the giving up of personal desires in order to follow the will of God – even if that meant the losing of one's life. In his discourse at the last supper he states it unequivocally:

This is my commandment:
love one another,
as I have loved you.
A man can have no greater love
than to lay down his life for his friends. (John 15:12–13)

This was the kind of man that Jesus was – a man who poured his life out in the service of others and, when it came to the crunch, gave his life for his friends. Had Jesus been simply a good man, like Gandhi, or Archbishop Oscar Romero, then his life would have been truly admirable. What we are asked to take on board, however, is that this Galilean carpenter was also God. How great then, was his descent amongst us. As Paul puts it:

> His state was divine,
>   yet he did not cling
> to his equality with God
> but emptied himself
> to assume the condition of a slave,
> and became as men are;
> and being as all men are,
> he was humbler yet,
> even to accepting death,
>   death on a cross. (Phil. 2:6–8)

This is a key passage in understanding the nature of Christ because it describes his *kenosis*, his emptying out, his total self-giving. It was this ideal, this way of living and being, that Jesus tried so hard to teach his disciples. On that last night he told them again and again:

> 'My little children, . . .
>   I give you a new commandment:
> love one another;
> just as I have loved you,
> you also must love one another.
> By this love you have for one another,
> everyone will know that you are my disciples.' (John
>   13:33–5)

In a last desperate effort to get through to them that both he and they were called to serve, not to rule, he stripped off his shirt and, tying a towel around his waist, washed his disciples' feet. That this was no ordinary gesture can be seen from Peter's astonished reaction: 'Lord,

I couldn't possibly let *you* wash my feet.' Jesus' reply, however, was quite clear: if Peter refused to participate in this ceremony, this role play, he could have nothing in common with Jesus.

It is difficult to understand why Jesus felt so strongly about this – until we realize that he was trying to teach them not only his own way, but the way of his Father, the unknown, transcendent God. Again and again, Jesus tried to get through to these simple men the truth of his union with the Father. When Philip, at the last supper, said to Jesus: 'Lord, let us see the Father, and then we shall be satisfied', Jesus replied in exasperation:

'Have I been with you all this time, Philip, and still you
 do not know me?
To have seen me is to have seen the Father,
So how can you say, "Let us see the Father"?
Do you not believe
that I am in the Father and the Father is in me?' (John
 14:9–10)

How difficult it is for us to understanding this mystery. No wonder the full impact of it escapes us. I find the passage from Philippians 2, the *kenosis* passage, helpful, for Paul tells us that not only did Jesus empty himself and assume the condition of a slave, but that God rewarded him precisely because of this:

But God raised him high
 and gave him the name
which is above all other names
so that *all beings*
in the heavens, on earth and in the underworld,
should bend the knee at the name of Jesus
and that every tongue should acclaim

Jesus Christ as Lord,
    to the glory of God the Father. (Phil. 2:9–11)

So here we have the gerat Christian paradox: that Christ's kingship is not in spite of his humiliation and suffering but because of it. By pouring himself out like water, by giving away everything he had, including his life, he was behaving in a God-like way. This is what I mean when I say that Christ revealed the nature of God by the death he died: he showed for all to see that God, the transcendent creator God, has chosen to be powerless, to be empty, for his people. He is a weak and suffering God, because his love makes him vulnerable to betrayal and rejection. He is, I suppose, quite simply a God who loves too much, a God who makes a fool of himself.

Paul had a deep sense of the foolishness of the message that he was called to preach:

> The language of the cross may be illogical to those who are not on the way to salvation, but those of us who are on the way see it as God's power to save. . . And so, while the Jews demand miracles and the Greeks look for wisdom, here are we preaching a crucified Christ; to the Jews an obstacle that they cannot get over, to the pagans madness, but to those who have been called, whether they are Jews or Greeks, a Christ who is the power and the wisdom of God. For God's foolishness is wiser than human wisdom, and God's weakness is stronger than human strength. (1 Cor. 1:18, 22–5)

I find this foolish God wonderfully attractive. How could one be afraid of a God like that? In awe, yes, but afraid, no. This is the God I find again and again in the Old Testament. We meet him in Hosea, the betrayed husband who pursues his adulterous wife into the desert in order to speak lovingly to her heart, or the God who cries out to his thirsty people:

> Come to the water, all you who are thirsty;
>   though you have no money, come! (Isa. 55:1)

This is the God who sees himself not as all-powerful ruler but as husband and lover:

> For the mountains may depart,
>   the hills be shaken,
>   but my love for you will never leave you. (Isa. 54:10)

A few months ago, while on retreat, I was given the Isaiah passage about the water and the story of the Samarian woman at the well to read. What struck me about both of these passages was the tremendous urgency with which God is calling us. When Jesus speaks to the Samarian woman he says: 'If only you *knew* what God was offering you!' I suddenly had a new image of God: that of a man or woman in a wheelchair – a powerless God, calling out wistfully to those he loved, hoping that they would come to him.

This, it seems to me, is the God we are shown today, the God hanging on the cross. He is a weak and foolish God, besotted with love, calling out to us. I wonder, can we hear him? And it is this same powerless God who, by entering our world, taking on our vulnerable flesh, has redeemed us. Jesus is the foolish one who has become a scapegoat on our behalf. As Isaiah says of the suffering servant:

> But we, we thought of him as someone punished,
>   struck by God and brought low.

Yet he was pierced through for our faults,
crushed for our sins.
On him lies a punishment that brings us peace,
    and through his wounds we are healed. (Isa.
    53:4–5)

It is this passage from Isaiah which foretells the amazing
mystery of the redemption – that in some way that we can
only guess at, Christ by his suffering has taken upon
himself the sins of our world: the violence of the soldier
who rapes, the cruelty of the torturer, the callousness of
the youth who mugs an old lady for her pension. I do
not claim to understand it, but I know that this act somehow holds our world together.

Paul, in his letter to the Colossians, adds another
dimension to the story. He is glad to suffer, he says,
because he makes up in his own body what is wanting,
lacking, in the sufferings of Christ. Once again I do not
pretend to understand this cryptic statement, but I find
it enormously comforting, for if Paul believes that his
suffering is somehow taken up in Christ's then surely so
is the suffering of all of us. I have come to believe that
all suffering is in some way redemptive, that therein lies
its meaning. The grief and humiliation of the Romanian
orphans or the brutalized women of Bosnia are not
wasted. Somehow their terrible pain has a purpose, is
used in the divine economy.

So, as we contemplate Christ upon his cross let us be
mindful not just of the God who loved us so much that
he became man and died for us, but also of all the men
and women in whom Christ lives on. Let us weep for
them and remember that somehow our lives are connec-
ted, that on them lies the punishment that makes us
whole and that by their wounds we are healed.

5

Good Friday:
the Mystery of Redemption

WHEN I WAS a little girl at school, learning my catechism, one of the questions we were asked was, 'Why do we call that day *good* on which Christ died?'

Curiously enough, I can remember the question but not the answer – probably because I didn't really understand it. But it's a good question, one that we should ask ourselves today – because if we can arrive at an answer we have found the cornerstone, the essential truth upon which the whole edifice of the Christian faith is built. I find the following passage from Colossians very helpful in understanding the meaning of Good Friday:

> It makes me happy to suffer for you, as I am suffering now, and in my own body to do what I can to make up all that has still to be undergone by Christ for the sake of his body, the Church. I became the servant of the Church when God made me responsible for delivering God's message to you, the message which was a mystery hidden for generations and centuries and has now been revealed to his saints. It was God's purpose to reveal it to them and to show all the rich glory of this mystery to pagans. The mystery is Christ among you, your hope of glory; this

is the Christ we proclaim, this is the wisdom in which
we thoroughly train everyone and instruct everyone,
to make them all perfect in Christ. It is for this I
struggle wearily on, helped only by his power driving
me irresistibly. (Col. 1:24–9)

There are two things which I take from this passage.
The first is the paradox of Paul's happiness; he declares
that he is happy to suffer for the sake of the Good News.
We need to think for a moment what Paul's life was like.
It wasn't just that he was a workaholic, that he drove
himself on and on, but he was physically persecuted,
imprisoned, beaten and ultimately executed. Either Paul
was crazy, or it must have been *some* message that he was
preaching.

We know of course that although Paul was driven he
wasn't in the least bit crazy. So, what exactly was, is, this
message that he and so many others have been prepared
to die for? And what has happened to us that the fire has
gone out of our faith? The message is contained in Paul's
words; it is quite clear, but so simple, so familiar that we
miss it. 'The mystery is Christ among you, your hope of
glory.' Christ among us – what does it *mean*? It's here
that we must move beyond the cross to the resurrection,
because the cross is not the end. Although Jesus the Son
of God died on the cross – as people still die under
torture today – he rose again and is here amongst us. Our
God is not a distant out-there God, but Emmanuel, God
with us. He is here with us *now*, inside you and me. The
emptiness of God – which somehow *is* God – the
unformed, mysterious, transcendent creator God is with
us, filling our own emptiness, his deep calling to ours,
yearning to be united within us, to fill us with abundant
life.

This is the mystery for which the martyrs died: that the

God who made us, the mysterious uncreated God, became flesh and lived among us as a real human person. And when he died, when we killed him, he rose again from the dead. But not only that. By his death on the cross and his rising again he has set us free: he has conquered the death which we all fear so much. This is what we mean when we say that Christ, by his holy cross, has redeemed the world: he has rescued us from the state of bondage into which we were born.

The second point that I take from this passage is Paul's statement that he is doing what he can to make up in his own body 'all that still has to be undergone by Christ for the sake of his body the Church'. These lines are enormously important to me because I believe that Paul is saying that his sufferings are somehow joined with Christ's and are therefore redemptive. It's not that God's suffering wasn't *enough* to ransom us – but that, because Christ exists in a time different from our own, in eternal time, and because he lives in us and we in him, his sufferings and ours are intertwined. So the sufferings of the people of our own day, of the Christs of Latin America, of Central Europe, or of our own land, are inextricably caught up with the sufferings of God. This means that they, like he, are suffering servants – pierced through for our faults, crushed for our sins. On them lies a punishment that brings *us* peace and through *their* wounds we are healed.

This idea that all suffering is somehow redemptive has helped me enormously in my work with the dying. However terrible, however apparently meaningless a particular situation seems, I believe that there *is* meaning in it. I believe therefore that no suffering is wasted, that no tears are lost. As it says in the psalms, all of our suffering is recorded in God's book, all of our tears saved in his bottle. I like to think that perhaps these tears are used to water the arid, desert hearts of those who do not know God or do not care for his people. Perhaps the tears of the Romanian orphans will somehow contribute towards healing the bitterness of the divisions in former Yugoslavia. Who knows! We can only pray and trust that God will, in his own good time, rescue his people.

This image of Christ the rescuer was a very popular one in the early Church and led to the wonderful story of the harrowing of hell, a sort of alternative version of the resurrection. The story, which is a fantasy built upon the gospels, begins with Jesus' death, when, as Matthew tells us:

> the veil of the Temple was torn in two from top to bottom; the earth quaked; the rocks were split; the tombs opened and the bodies of many holy men rose from the dead, and these, after his resurrection, came out of the tombs, entered the Holy City and appeared to a number of people. (Matt. 27:51–3)

In the early days of the Church – around AD 500 and something – a document was written called the 'Gospel of Nicodemus'. This apocryphal gospel tells the story that two of the sons of Simeon (the high priest from whom we get the *Nunc Dimittis*) were raised from the dead in the great cosmic upheaval after Jesus died. When they heard this, the high priests Annas and Caiaphas and the Jewish elders Nicodemus, Joseph and Gamaliel went and sought them out and brought them to the temple and asked them to write down what had happened to them, and this is the story they told:

These two men were in Hades, in the underworld prison of the dead, with Adam and Eve, Simeon, John the Baptist, the prophets and all the good men who had died before Jesus. Now although Hades was not a place of fiery torment like hell, it was still a very terrible place –

grey and bleak and lifeless, like a prison camp or an old-style insane asylum. The people who were confined there were all without hope, depressed and lifeless, like the men and women of Auschwitz, the chronically insane or people with far-advanced Alzheimer's disease.

As the prisoners sat there in the darkness of their prison they suddenly felt the heat and the light of the sun. They were amazed; their hearts stirred and they began to wonder what on earth was happening. The propet Isaiah spoke first. 'I remember', he said, 'that when I was on earth I prophesied: "The people that walked in darkness has seen a great light; on those who live in a land of deep shadow, a light has shone." '

Then Zachary, father of the Baptist, spoke: 'I remember speaking about the light shining upon those who sit in darkness and the shadow of death.' Then, as they struggled to make sense of what was happening to them, Satan arrived in Hades and said to the keeper of the prison: 'Guess what, we persuaded the Jews to kill Jesus.' Hades, however, was appalled. 'You fool,' he said. 'Don't you realize that we could never contain Jesus down here. Look at what happened to his friend Lazarus – he leaped like an eagle from the tomb.' Then, even as they talked, there was a noise outside the prison, a noise like an army. Bar the gates, shouted Hades – but it was too late. There was a brilliant light, and the gates of hell splintered like matchwood as the victorious Christ entered using his cross like a battering ram to knock the doors down.

This story has been the subject of icons and frescoes for well over a thousand years. The earliest one we know of dates from the seventh century and is in the Church of Santa Maria Antiqua in Rome. The one that I like best is a fresco in the church of the Chora in Istanbul. I have christened it 'Christ the Fireman' because it shows an amazingly virile Christ grabbing a limp Adam and Eve by the wrists and hauling them bodily out of hell. It's as though he was an SAS man rescuing two hostages or a fireman dragging two unconscious bodies from a burning building just before it collapses.

This is the way I see resurreciton and our own transition from death to new life, from capture to freedom. I believe that somehow, as we die, whether we die quietly in our beds or with terrible violence on the road or in a war, that Christ the Fireman is there, at that moment, and we are swept out of the jaws of death and into the arms of God.

6

Christct the Fireman

'O COMFORT my people,' sing the monks every Advent.

> O comfort my people and calm all their fear
>> And tell them the time of salvation is near . . .
> All mountains and hills shall become as a plain,
> For vanished are mourning and hunger and pain,
> Never again shall these war against you,
>> Behold, I come quickly to make all things new.

I know this is an Advent hymn, rejoicing at the coming
of the Messiah, but sometimes I think we should sing it
in Holy Week too, to remind ourselves that our Avenger
liveth, that Christ the Fireman, the rescuer, is about to be
born from the wounded flank of the dead Jesus.

Holding oneself together theologically in Holy Week
takes a bit of doing. We are plunged ever deeper into
the passion, gazing upon the sacred head ill used, the
disfigured features of the man of sorrows, caught up in
the horror of unsolicited violence, man's appalling inhu-
manity. And even if we have no time or heart to contemplate the sacred mysteries, they are splashed unrelentingly
every day on our television screens. Christ dies in Bosnia,
in Belfast, in Warrington. He is a Muslim woman raped
and bleeding, a schoolboy blown to pieces by bombs and

a toddler tied to a railway track. Father forgive them, for they know not what they do.

These are the mysteries we should be pondering each Good Friday, not trying vainly to imagine how Jesus looked as he climbed the hill to Golgotha. We know well enough what he looked like: like any desperate Kurd or Slav, stumbling barefoot over mountain paths, eyes blinded by tears, shoulders bowed with fatigue. He looked like the youngster I ignored yesterday in the street, a bedraggled booted teenager, sitting hopelessly on the pavement clutching a mongrel puppy, her face contorted with emptiness and pain. We know what he looked like; what we need to learn is how to comfort him suffering here and now. Jesus Christ, son of the living God, have mercy on us, have mercy on them. Show us what we should do. Give us diviners of living water lest we die of thirst.

But he *has* given us diviners of the water of life, and we do not recognize them. We ignore today's prophets because they are unshaven pop stars like Bob Geldof, scruffy missionaries from Latin America, or Indian-skirted social workers talking of child abuse and the death of the inner city. It is so much easier to believe that some are born wicked than that most have wickedness thrust upon them. The frustrated, sex-starved father who visits his girl child under cover of darkness produces a woman so hurt that she may never relate fully to husband or child. Desperate for a love never known, she will likely go from one man to another, bearing unwanted, unloved and rejected children: another generation of wounded and wounding people. Lord, where are we to find a way out of this terrible cycle of pain? Why is it so much easier to say: 'Flog them! Shoot them! Crucify him! Crucify him!'

But what of the victims? What hope is there for our rejected street people, for the shop-soiled refugee bearing

an unwanted, bastard child? Does hatred cross the pla-
cental barrier? What will happen to these children begot-
ten in violence? Will the divine spark catch fire in them,
or lie for ever dormant? Will these babies be tossed into
a bleak orphanage, doomed to stand and rock on the
bars of their prison cots like animals in a cage? The
answer, I suppose, is yes, probably many of them will.
But, please God, this tragedy will be the spur to another
movement of love, set on fire the hearts of suburban
women, nurses and mothers so that they will go to the
rescue of other women's children.

This, it seems to me, is one of the great paradoxes of
our world: that so often we need tragedy to draw us out
of the torpor of our well-ordered lives. The blood of
martyrs is the seedbed of the faith. Today's nurses are the
children of the women who attended the horror of
the Crimea, and legions of counsellors have been brought
into existence because of appalling tragedies like the
King's Cross fire or the wrecking of a British ferry boat.
This is the way our world is: we are groaning, as Paul puts
it, in a mighty travail, struggling to give birth to the good
implanted in all of us and in this fair green earth. See,
the green blade riseth, Love has come again.

I seem, this Holy Week, more than ever conscious of
my own labour pains and the birthing agony of the world
around me, for I have spent much of the past few days in
tears. Attending, quite innocently, a course on how to
teach 'communication skills', I found myself plunged into
role play and groupwork with all the heady emotion that
this kind of enterprise sometimes generates. Absurdly sensitive to the slightest criticism and all but deaf to positive
feedback, I burst regularly into tears and had difficulty in
carrying on. In hindsight, I feel as if some hard carapace
had been split open and my vulnerability laid bare. Now
that it is over and I sit licking my wounds, I know that

this has been a week of singular growth. Why could I not have learned this stuff from a book, I ask myself? Why did I have nearly to die of shame? Perhaps it was because my own arrogant devils could only be driven out by the experience of pain and humiliation. Perhaps this was yet another of those little deaths which have to be died if one is to continue upon the road to the Golgotha of being fully human.

Even as I write these last words I wonder if they are blasphemous; but perhaps we can only move towards being fully human as our harness is smitten piece by painful piece from our aching shoulders. 'Naked I wait thy love's uplifted stroke,' wrote Francis Thompson in 'The Hound of Heaven': 'faileth now even dream the dreamer, and the lute the lutanist'. Perhaps Irenaeus, when he wrote that the glory of God is a human being fully alive, was writing not of some muscle-bound suntanned Adonis but of the countless broken Christ figures letting go of life. The drowning teenager, hand loosening on the upturned canoe, is both sinking into the oblivion of death and bursting through the veil that separates us from eternity. The writer of the fifth-century gospel of Nicodemus captures the paradox of death as the key to life when he writes of Lazarus, four days dead, corrupt and stinking in the grave, yet 'shaking himself like an eagle' and leaping forth from the tomb, with 'all agility and swiftness'.

I think I have always known, deep down, that death is also birth, but last year, in Istanbul, I took another step toward understanding the Christian roots of my faith. Visiting, tourist-like, the ancient church of the Chora, I found myself gazing spellbound at the icon, or rather the fresco, of the Harrowing of Hell. High on the apse of the central part of the church is the figure that I have christened 'Christ the Fireman', immense and vigorous, striding to the rescue of the prisoners in hell with all the power of a commando. This is no pale Galilean of the story books but El Salvador, Christ the Saviour, battering down the Bastille doors of Hades and grasping Adam and Eve by their limp and drowning wrists and dragging them to safety. After him in a great swelling crowd come David the poet, the lean and swarthy Baptist, ancient Zachary and the prophet Isaiah. And after them, if I see clearly without my spectacles, come the raped and the tortured, the car-smashed and the crumbled old. It is precisely at this moment of apparent extinction, it seems to me, that we are born again into a life of unimagined joy. As the last shell is split off and the pieces fall about us, we rise, shining and new, into that life for which we were created.

This then is what Easter tells us: that without pain there can be no growth, without loss no finding, and without death no leap into the heart of God.

7

How Blest the Sorrowful

How blest are the sorrowful, for they shall find consolation (Matt. 5:4 NEB)

IT SEEMS TO ME that there have been three distinct stages in my encounter with the beatitudes, three different levels of engagement and understanding. The first level was the easiest, the cosiest and the most superficial; it is the level of appreciation of the poetry, the counterpoint and the paradox. At first hearing one thinks, 'How lovely, how reassuring, how true'; one's heart warms and one feels comforted. And that is good – for the words *are* beautiful and poetic and true, and have a power to lift the heart.

The second encounter came to me many years later, when I had the courage to question words and concepts which I had always accepted simply because they were in the gospel. It came at a time when I was split wide open by the terrible reality of suffering: by the hunger of the Third World, the pain and impotence of the oppressed and the weariness and despair of the incurably sick. These were in truth, the sorrowful: the Ethiopian woman whose shrunken breasts were a dried-up water hole for her dying baby; the man held head down in a bath of filth because he would not betray his friends; and the doctor aged twenty-two with a brain tumour, cut off like a wild flower as her face was turned towards the sun. Who dares call these people blest, for when and in what green lands will they find consolation? Will the relief workers arrive in time to save the Ethiopian woman? Will her breasts fill again with milk and her baby gurgle with delight? Or will she, like thousands of others, drop silently to the ground, too weak even to weep for the dead child in her arms? Will her bones whiten in the sun alongside those of the cattle, a silent witness to the harshness of nature, the immutability of bureaucracy and monstrous injustice of a divided world? And what of the freedom-fighter, the guerrilla, the revolutionary? Will the excrement in his lungs be replaced by clean air, or will he too die of pneumonia, his ribs kicked in and his hands crushed by interrogators blinded by fear, hatred and indoctrination?

And what of the fat cats, the politicians, the generals, the businessmen in their capital cities, racked by a sorrow so deep they cannot even touch it, cannot name it, a sorrow that can only be expressed as greed and a lust for power. When, and in what time and place, will *they* find consolation? Or will they remain for ever hungry, manipulators of men, blind to the sun and the stars unil they plunge deeper and deeper into the pit of their own avarice and stupidity?

And the sick, the handicapped, the broken, so much more accessible to us in the 'developed' world: will their cancers vanish, the pain go, their mutilated bodies be restored to wholeness? Will they leap for joy and dance again – or will they fade, their limbs shrunken and their bellies swollen until they are indistinguishable from the Ethiopian, the prisoner and the refugee? When will their mourning be turned into joy, their sorrow into consolation? Today? Tomorrow? In heaven – or never? Do the beatitudes promise hope of resurrection – or pie in the sky to comfort the bystanders, release us from the pain of responsibility, of solidarity, of being a member of the human race? I have no answers to these awkward, almost blasphemous questions, save the conviction that they must be asked. If we Christians do not ask them, the unbelievers certainly will, and there can be no meeting point unless we have the courage for dialogue.

My first experience of such questioning began in prison when I was joined in the solitary confinement block of a Santiago prison by a girl of nineteen called Lelia. Highly intelligent and a Marxist, with a mind far more open and enquiring than my own, Lelia was determined to put her captivity to good use. Quite unashamedly, she set about me, not to convert, but to learn what I believed. What was this Christianity about? What use was it to turn the other cheek – was this not just capitalistic propaganda to keep the poor in their place, to stop them from rising up to claim their rightful inheritance? I can't remember how I handled her questions, only that I struggled to answer honestly in my broken Spanish and squirmed at the forthrightness of her questioning. I remember too that I loved her, so young, so honest, so serious – and so given to the poor of her land.

My own experience of questioning, however, came much later when I began to work with the dying. For me, reflection and questioning of my faith came very late, and I experienced a certain degree of wheel-wobble. A period of stress and depression led me into conversation with a psychologist and, as I explored the forces that drive me, I was forced to question my own personal salvation history and the belief that God had called me to his exclusive service from my youth. As I pieced together the fragments of memory of a wartime childhood and an adolescence marked by hero-worship of nuns and priests, I realized that my 'vocation' had a very human basis to it as well as,

if not instead of, a divine. With my foundations thus
rocked, I turned slowly to face the whole of my belief
system, wondering if it would collapse like some
elaborate card house and leave me weeping amidst the
ruins.

For a while, I sat in the fog, becalmed, lost, literally not
knowing if I believed in God or not. At forty-seven I was
plunged into adolescent questioning, wondering if the
cynical jest, 'and in the beginning, man created God',
could possibly be true. There is no dramatic beginning
or end to my agnostic period – it came upon me gradually
like a patch of mist and lifted just as unexpectedly a few
months later. It has left me, as I have heard other people
say, believing less but with more conviction, though that
conviction itself is a fragile thing and pure gift. Like this
poet, I can say:

> Barely I believe yet truly,
>   God is one and God is Three,
> God is love and seen most fully,
> Hanging from the wintry Tree,
> And I trust Creator Spirit,
> In and through our common life,
> Weaving threads all torn and broken,
> shaping justice out of strife.
>
> And I cherish – with due patience –
> For the sake of God alone,
> Words and Folk of inspiration,
> And the Sacraments Christ's own.
>
> I embrace the Law of Loving,
> Dying to possessive need,
> Risen with Christ,

[71]

Though crushed by wine press,
            Into spacious glory breathed.*

'Risen with Christ, though crushed by wine press.' What
does he mean? Is he speaking simply of the life after
death, a life beyond starvation, torture or cancer – or of
some liberty of the spirit attainable in this life, in spite
of – perhaps even because of – suffering, mourning, the
crushing between the forces of fate, injustice or disease?
I don't know, but I think it has to be both. Just as there
is no doubt that some people emerge from suffering to a
life of new liberty of spirit, so others are apparently
crushed by it, submerged under the weight of bitterness
and pain. It seems crucial to me that 'believing' people
could have the courage to face this aspect of human
experience, for to pretend that all are strengthened, puri-
fied and liberated by suffering is to be quite out of touch
with reality. And a Christianity which is not firmly rooted
in reality is not Christianity at all.

When I embarked upon this piece, I had thought to
find clear and powerful words about the consolation of
the sorrowful. Surely I who have emerged strengthened
from the torture chamber and who am in daily contact
with the dying must have some answers to the problems
of suffering? And yet, when the moment comes, I find
myself almost empty-handed. What I offer is a disjointed
series of reflections, which may or may not make sense.

The first thing I would say is that I don't really understand what 'blest' implies. Some translations render it as
'happy'. Are we to understand this word in its literal sense,
or are we talking about some deep spiritual happiness
inaccessible at the level of the feelings? God knows, I was

* Jim Cotter, in *Healing More or Less*, Cairns Publications.

not happy in the torture cell nor am I when in the midst of the black moods of despair which plague me from time to time. Jean Vanier understands 'blest' as being somehow specially watched over by God. That I find easier to accept, for I have experienced the presence of God in the midst of atrocious suffering.

During the experience of torture in which intolerable pain was compounded by terror and powerlessness, I was aware of the presence of God in quite a curious way: I felt he was there, alongside, somehow in solidarity with me and yet not taking the pain away. He was just there – not comforting or protecting, but there. In the midst of the squalor of the interrogation centre with its harsh guards and filthy lavatories I was no longer an onlooker at the passion but somehow taking part. It was not a great mystical experience – just a rather matter-of-fact appreciation of a reality.

Later on, in solitary confinement, I met God in a quite different way. The torture was apparently over, although I lived in constant terror that the interrogators would begin again. My days were spent in a small room containing two sets of bunks and a chair. I saw the warders briefly when they brought the food or when they let me out to go to the lavatory. Otherwise I was left alone to my thoughts, my fears and whatever prayers I was capable of.

Now, twelve years later, I believe that this three-week period of struggle and desolation was of crucial importance, for I see it as a time of naked encounter with God. Like Jacob, I wrestled all night with an unseen stranger and was somehow blest before he left me, wounded, at daybreak.

> And Jacob was left alone. And there was one that wrestled with him until daybreak who, seeing that he could not master him, struck him in the socket of

his hip, and Jacob's hip was dislocated as he wrestled with him. He said 'Let me go, for day is breaking'. But Jacob answered, 'I will not let you go unless you bless me'. He then asked, 'What is your name?' 'Jacob,' he replied. He said, 'Your name shall no longer be Jacob, but Israel; because you have been strong against God, you shall prevail against men'. Jacob then made this request, 'I beg you, tell me your name', but he replied, 'Why do you ask my name?' And he blessed him there.

Jacob named the place Peniel, 'because I have seen God face to face,' he said, 'and I have survived'. (Gen. 32:24–31)

Some years ago I came across a quotation from a nineteenth-century philosopher called Stifter. He wrote: 'Pain is a Holy Angel which shows treasure to men which otherwise remains forever hidden.' I knew at once what he meant and that it was true, although it is one of those mysterious truths which is difficult to explain to others. Dare we say that those who mourn are blest because they encounter God in a special way, that Stifter's Holy Angel reveals to them a treasure which remains hidden to those whose life takes a smoother, apparently happier course? I believe that this is true, though I am not sure if I can explain why.

What did I learn during those three weeks alone?

> That night, that year
> Of now done darkness I wretch lay wrestling with (my God!) my God.
> (Gerard Manley Hopkins, 'Carrion Comfort')

Perhaps I should explain a little about the nature of my struggle, which could, I think, be described in spiritual jargon as an abandonment experience. Although what happened to me occurred in the rather exotic context of a South American gaol, it is, in essence, the same struggle undergone by many people who find themselve trapped by illness or unfortunate personal circumstances. The experience is not about prison *per se* but about a way of confronting and adapting to a situation from which there is no escape.

After the initial nightmare days of the torture centre where I survived from minute to minute, sometimes cowering like a frightened animal and sometimes given powers of endurance that astonished me, I was transferred to another hidden prison called Cuatro Alamos (Four Poplars), the solitary confinement block. As the door slammed on me and I found myself alone, I at last had space to think. When the first twenty-four hours elapsed without further interrogation and my most primitive needs of food and sleep were satisfied, I was free to explore the limits of my inner freedom. Denied more than a few square feet for physical manoeuvre, I found that my spiritual space was much larger. It was not long before I found myself reciting Lovelace's poem:

> Stone walls do not a prison make,
>   Nor iron bars a cage;
> Minds innocent and quiet take,
>   That for an hermitage;
> If I have freedom in my love
> And in my soul am free,
> Angels alone, that soar above,
>   Enjoy such liberty.*

In this secret space I found that I had two very clear options. The first was to pray to be let out, and the second

* Richard Lovelace, 'To Althea, from Prison'.

was to accept whatever God had in mind for me. In human terms, of course, this was Hobson's Choice – the Lord does whatever he wills, anyway – but in spiritual and psychological terms, the difference it made was enormous. If we scream to be let out we are like a wild bird in a cage, beating our wings aginst the bars until we are terrified, bruised and exhausted. All our energy is dissipated in the fight, and we are left spent and useless. If we are able to accept, however, and to trust, then not only do we enter into a quite different relationship with God, but we are able to use our psychic energy in a creative rather than in a destructive way.

So this was my battle: between praying to be released and praying for the strength to accept God's Will. It was a drama enacted over the three weeks of my confinement, for although on some days I was able to make an act of acceptance, at other moments I was reduced again to despair and the plea that the cup should be taken from me. My deepest fears were that I should be executed or confined to prison for many years, and I was terrified at either prospect. And yet, eventually, I was able to let go, and say, 'Thy will be done.'

Some time during the course of my solitary confinement, I received a visit from the British consul who brought me a parcel from my friends. Among the gifts of clothes, soap and chocolate was E. F. Farrell's book, *Disciples and Other Strangers*, which contained in its appendix the following poem:

ABANDONMENT

Father,
I abandon myself into your hands . . .
What does it mean to abandon oneself to God?
What is an abandonment experience?

Is it leaving oneself on God's doorstep,
    walking into the rest of life,
        not allowing anxiety,
            fear,
            frustration to enter into one?
Is it expecting God to keep one warm,
            secure,
            and safe,
            unharmed?
Is that abandonment?

Abandonment has nothing to do with warmth of
            womb or arms
            or closed clasped hearts.

It is not something done by a child.
It is done to him.
It cannot be done to an adult.
It is done by him.
Abandonment is committed only with and in the
    maturity of Christ Jesus.
It is not just a hanging loose.
It is a letting go.
It is a severing of the strings by which one manipulates,
        controls,
        administrates
      the forces in one's life
Abandonment is managing nothing,
        blocking or blotting out nothing,
        expecting nothing.
Abandonment is receiving all things the way one receives
        a gift
        with opened hands,
        an opened heart.

Abandonment to God
    Is the climactic point in any man's life.

There is nothing left to do then.
No place to go.
Death has occurred.*

What happens during an abandonment experience? In what sense is it the climactic point in a person's life? Again, I find it difficult to explain, except to say that one enters into a new relationship with God – that like Jacob, though wounded, one is somehow blest. Perhaps the essence is the transference of the knowledge that God loves us from the level of the intellect to that of the guts. Like Mother Julian, one knows somehow that, whatever happens, all things shall be well and all manner of things shall be well. One knows that God is there, with one, in fear and danger, in desolation and despair. This is the consolation of those that mourn – they know that God is somehow in their pain and darkness, that they do not walk alone.

It is important to undertand that this carnal knowledge of God brings consolation at a level so deep that we can barely touch it, for it is a consolation that can and does coexist with fear, anxiety, depression and unhappiness. This is one of the great mysteries of the spiritual life: that although closeness to God is a source of unimaginable joy, it does not in any sense protect us from the pain which is an integral part of the human condition. We remain the people we always were, neurotic and fragile, subject to anger, self-pity and dark despair. And yet, there

---

* Anonymous, in E. J. Farrell, *Disciples and Other Strangers*, Dimension Books (USA) 1976.

is a difference, which I think is manifested as the virtue of hope. A monk friend of mine makes the distinction between *expectation* and *hope*. *Expectation* is that which is likely to happen, given the way things are: a cure is likely, or things can only get worse. *Hope*, on the other hand, is the knowledge that God can and will bring good out of evil, light out of darkness, life out of death. Hope is the basis of Bonhoeffer's statement:

> I believe that God can and will bring good out of evil. For that purpose he needs men who make the best use of everything. I believe God will give us all the power we need to resist in times of distress. But he never gives it in advance, lest we should rely upon ourselves and not upon him alone.*

I find it fascinating to hear Bonhoeffer, the twentieth-century Lutheran pastor imprisoned in Nazi Germany, echoing the words of another German, the fourteenth-century Dominican mystic, Meister Eckhart. In one of his sermons Eckhart writes boldly of the God who deliberately strips his servants of all their supports and props so that they may rest on him alone.

> The faithful God often lets his friends fall sick and lets every prop on which they lean be knocked out from under them. It is a great joy to loving people to be able to do important things such as watching, fasting and the like, besides sundry more difficult undertakings. In such things they find their joy, their stay and their hope. Thus their pious works are supports, stays, footings to them.
> Our Lord wants to take all these things away, for

* Dietrich Bonhoeffer, *Letters and Papers from Prison*, SCM Press 1953.

he would like to be their only stay. He does this because of his simple goodness and mercy. He wants nothing more than his own goodness. He will not be influenced in the least to give or do by any act of ours. Our Lord wants his friends to be rid of such notions. That is why he removes every prop, so that he alone may support them. It is his will to give greatly, but only because of his own free goodness, so that he shall be their support and they, finding themselves to be nothing at all, may know how great the generosity of God is. For the more helpless and destitute the mind that turns to God for support can be, the deeper the person penetrates God and the more sensitive he is to God's most valuable gifts. Man must build on God alone.*

I do not know whether Eckhart is right and whether God deliberately exposes some people to sufferings in order to strengthen them. There is certainly ample precedent for this line of thought in the Old Testament if one considers the story of Job or the Wisdom literature:

My son, if you aspire to serve the Lord,
prepare yourself for an ordeal.
    Be sincere of heart, be steadfast,
and do not be alarmed when disaster comes.
Cling to him and do not leave him,
so that you may be honoured at the end of your days.
Whatever happens to you, accept it,
and in the uncertainties of your humble state, be patient,
since gold is tested in the fire,
    and chosen men in the furnace of humiliation.
    (Ecclesiasticus 2:1–5)

* Meister Eckhart, Sermon 19.

If we accept as mystery that perhaps God does test some men in the 'furnace of humiliation' we can go on to explore the spiritual and psychological mechanisms by which disaster can be seen, in hindsight, as gift. I have scandalized many people by saying that I see my prison experiences as a gift – and perhaps I have unconsciously denied the horror of it in order to escape the pain. Be that as it may, I believe that the experience of being stripped of all one's support systems has two profound effects. The first is that it does in truth force one to rest upon God alone, and the second is that it teaches one to understand as gift many things hitherto taken for granted. There is a very real sense in which the poor have the earth for their heritage, for when one is stripped of freedom, health, good food, possessions, one rediscovers what a monk friend of mine calls 'the essential giveness of things'. Released from pain one becomes grateful not to hurt; released from hunger, one is grateful for bread and water. I recall hearing a woman who escaped from Auschwitz describe how she ate a tube of toothpaste and found it the most delicious thing she had ever tasted. In prison I found myself praying an extraordinary litany of thanksgiving – for my wholeness of body, for my food, my blanket, for the sparrows with whom I shared my crumbs and for the glimpse of the sunrise gained by standing on a chair at the window of my cell. Of course, one does not have to experience prison to learn to value the commonplace. So often one discovers that the most joyous and generous people are those who have experienced severe illness or bereavement.

On a recent visit to Corrymeela, a community for reconciliation in Northern Ireland, I met a remarkable woman who, after her son had been shot dead, emerged from her fury and grief to help other bereaved families. She went to the office of a Belfast newspaper, and made a list of the names and addresses of the people who had been killed, and began visiting their families. Almost without exception they greeted her with open arms, for they had had no one with whom they could talk through their anger and grief. From this beginning there grew a support group which still meets on a regular basis. I marvelled at this woman as she drove me to the airport. Here was someone whose mourning had been not turned into joy, but accompanied by it. Bonhoeffer captures it in his poem 'Sorrow and Joy':

Joy and Sorrow,
    hurled from the height of heaven in meteor
    fashion,
flash in an arc of shining menace o'er us.
Those they touch are left
stricken amid the fragments
    of their colourless, usual lives.

Imperturbable, mighty,
    ruinous and compelling,
Sorrow and Joy,
– summoned or all unsought for –
    processionally enter.

Those they encounter
    they transfigure, investing them
with strange gravity
    and a spirit of worship.*

* Dietrich Bonhoeffer, *Letters and Papers from Prison*, SCM Press 1953.

This, then, is my understanding of the truth that those who mourn shall find consolation. Specially blest by a God who loves the poor and the powerless, they struggle with him until daybreak. Then, having seen God face to face and survived, they emerge wounded but knowing deep in their guts that he loves them, that all his world is holy ground and that death, when it comes, is quite simply the beginning not the end.

8

Towards a Theology
of Hospice Care

IT IS ONE of the truisms of hospice philosophy that we must treat the 'whole person', body, mind and spirit. Dame Cicely Saunders, courageous pioneer of the modern hospice movement, speaks of *total pain*, by which she means that the physical agony of an individual may be compounded by fear of death, loss of independence, conflict with loved ones and a state of spiritual anguish in which faith is stretched to breaking-point and hope seems nothing but a child's fantasy. Those of us who work with the dying have learned long since that no one person can meet all these needs. We work in multi-disciplinary teams: doctors, nurses, social workers, chaplains, each contributing a particular expertise, trying to weave a seamless garment of loving care. It all sounds very neat and tidy: the doctors and nurses deal with the physical problems, the social worker with financial worries and family conflicts and the chaplain with the spiritual issues. Ordinary professionals cannot be expected to answer religious or philosophical questions; after all, we've had no training in theology or pastoral care. Who can blame us if we call for the chaplain when patients ask devastating questions like, 'Why me?' or, 'How can there be a loving God if he treats his people like this?'

Towards a Theology of Hospice Care

The trouble about the care of the dying, however, is that it is never neat and tidy. Cancer has no respect for internal boundaries, so that a palliative care doctor must be a jack of all trades, chest physician, psychiatrist, gynae-cologist and geriatric physician all in one. In the same way the physical and the psychological become inextri-cably mixed up, fear exacerbating pain and pain making people terribly afraid. Spiritual issues are likewise insepar-able from physical and psychological ones, for a depres-sive illness can induce a pathological sense of guilt and the resultant sense of unworthiness can make the person feel that they are beyond the reach of God's love and mercy. This phenomenon of total pain in the dying demands of carers not only that they work in teams, each respecting the other's contribution, but that they be, as far as is possible, 'total physicians', 'total nurses', and 'whole person chaplains'. By this I mean that doctors and nurses must be able to cope with the 'why me' ques-tions and chaplains must know where to find a vomit bowl and listen sympathetically to out-pouring of anguish about physical disintegration and increasing dependency. 'Shar-ing the darkness' of the dying demands that we share in the humiliation of the incontinent, the confusion of the demented as well as in the grey desolation of those whose faith no longer sustains them and whose hope has disappeared.

How then can we ordinary people meet the needs of our dying? What studies will prepare us to enter into their darkness and how are we to protect our own faith when confronted with unbearable suffering in friends or family or in the people with whom we work?

Peter Speck, chaplain and senior lecturer at the Royal Free Hospital in London, describes spiritual care as 'watching' with people, as Jesus' disciples watched with him in the garden that night before he died. We can 'watch', says Peter, 'through binoculars at a thousand paces', at a safe distance, without getting 'involved', too close for comfort – but of what use is that? As St James says, 'If one of the brothers or one of the sisters is in need of clothes and has not enough food to live on and one of you says to them, "I wish you well; keep yourselves warm and eat plenty," without giving them these bare necessities of life, then what good is that?' (James 2:15). In the same way, what use is it to say to someone, 'God bless you,' if we do not try to bring them God's love and peace with our own hands? True religion is this: visiting the sick, but not staying too long; listening rather than talking; looking after someone's cat, dog, canary; making long-distance phone calls; writing letters; doing washing, shopping, picking up mail. . . . The sick do not need to hear our pious platitudes but to meet God in us. Like the armless statue of Christ in the bombed French village, he has no hands but ours. If we are to accompany the dying, to watch *with* them rather than look *at* them, we need to prepare ourselves, to attend to our own agendas, professional, personal and spiritual. I believe that those of us who find ourselves called to spiritual ministry have an obligation in justice to do this 'work', for if we do not, we run the risk of giving inadequate care, of short-changing those who are already poor. To put Peter's statement in another way, the manner in which we respond to people's needs will depend upon four things: our knowledge, our skills, our spirituality and the person that we are.

There is a wide literature available on the medical and psychological knowledge and skills necessary for working with the terminally ill but little, as far as I know, about the spirituality and theology of the work. I would like, therefore, in the next few pages to try to define a theology of healthcare, and in particular a theology for those who work with the dying.

The first question that comes to mind is 'What is the difference between spirituality and theology? I thought at first that there must be a clear distinction and rang around my clerical friends to find it. To my surprise, however, there was no consensus. One Catholic priest friend saw theology as a rather arid, cerebral *knowing about* God, and spirituality as that very different *knowing* God in the intimacy of prayer and loving relationship. I understood what he meant but couldn't reconcile his definition with the way knowledge *about* God leads me to love him. My other friends assured me that there was no hard and fast distinction between the disciplines, and eventually I decided to settle for my own definition which is that our *spirituality* is the way we relate to God, where we meet him, what enlivens us spiritually. We may find ourselves drawn to a creation-centred spirituality, finding God in his universe, or we may, like Charles de Foucauld, yearn for the hidden, simple life of Jesus in Nazareth. Others may find God quite differently, in what is called the apophatic way, the way of unknowing. The poet R. S. Thomas writes with amazing passion of the unseen God, 'finding' him only in his absence, in his spoor, in the warm indentation of a bed just vacated or in the mystery of bird migration:

> He is that great void
>   we must enter, calling
> to one another on our way
> in the direction from which
> he blows. What matter
> if we should never arrive
> to breed or winter
> in the climate of our conception?

Enough we have been given wings
and a needle in the mind
to respond to his bleak north.
There are times even at the Pole
when he, too, pauses in his withdrawal,
    so that it is light there all night long.*

Clearly the 'bleak north' of God is not everyone's spirituality, but then neither is the concept of Jesus as brother, nor devotion to the Virgin of Lourdes, Guadalupe or Medjugorje. Spirituality is an intensely personal thing, and one person's treasured statue is another's kitsch.

Our spirituality, however, if it is to be more than a passing devotion, must be underpinned by theology, by an understanding of God. That understanding may be complex and cerebral or it may be the intuitive wisdom of the natural contemplative, but we must 'know', in so far as it is possible to know, what we believe and who it is we worship. In other words, what sort of a God do we believe in, what is our God concept?

I believe that our God concept, our understanding of God, is enormously important to how we approach spiritual care. If, for example, we see God as a harsh judge, intolerant of human weakness and the sins of the flesh, we will give different spiritual counsel than if we believe that God is an all-loving, all-forgiving, merciful father. How then do we acquire our knowledge of God? Have we drunk from clean wells ourselves, and have we learned to distinguish between the one true God and the counterfeits all around us?

*   *   *

* R. S. Thomas, 'Migrants', in *Mass for Hard Times*, Bloodaxe 1993.

It seems to me that there are three broad ways in which we acquire 'knowledge' of the unknowable God: through the teaching of others, through the scriptures and from God himself, herself. Let me put it another way: our knowledge of God is our *wisdom* and we acquire it through the wisdom of the Elders, the wisdom of the Word, and through Wisdom herself. This tidy division is, of course a totally artificial one, for the very word 'wisdom' is itself a poetic device used to convey not only certain attributes of the Divine, but the way in which unseen God is made manifest, revealed in our world. The teachings contained in the Old Testament wisdom literature are garnered from traditions both older and wider than those of the Hebrew scribes. In his fascinating *The Contemplative Face of Old Testament Wisdom*, John Eaton describes the ancient Egyptian concept of *Maat* which means 'order', 'truth', 'justice', and is personified as a female divinity.

> She is the thought of the Creator's heart and the utterance of his mouth. She is his companion, his daughter, and she is represented in the form of a girl bearing a feather on her head as a symbol of holiness. [How much less cumbersome than a veil!] She is the very life and food of gods and men, and the king is represented as offering a little image of her on the palm of his hand, stretched out to the Creator. . . .*

The king, the ruler, is pledged to love Maat and hate her opposite, which is chaos and lies. From his knowledge of Maat he issues laws which uphold order in the world and society.

* J. Eaton, *The Contemplative Face of Old Testament Wisdom*, SCM Press 1989.

Maat, therefore, unchanged since the beginning of things, thought of God and his Creating Word, is clearly the inspiration of the writers of the Old Testament wisdom literature:

> Yahweh created me when his purpose first unfolded,
>   before the oldest of his works.
> From everlasting I was firmly set,
> from the beginning, before earth came into being.
> The deep was not when I was born,
>   there were no springs to gush with water.
>
> I was by his side, a master craftsman,
>   delighting him day after day,
> ever at play in his presence,
> at play everywhere in his world,
> delighting to be with the sons of men. (Prov. 8: 22–4,
>   30–31)

I love the imagery of this feminine principle of God, his muse, his creative power, his joy bubbling over like a waterfall.

> She is a breath of the power of God,
>   pure emanation of the glory of the Almighty;
> She is a reflection of the eternal light,
> untarnished mirror of God's active power,
>   image of his goodness. (Wisd. 7:25–6)

It is this wisdom, this feminine 'reflection of the eternal light' that we are bidden to follow, like a will-o'-the-wisp in the fog. She dances tantalizingly in front of us, the fire at night, lighting the way amid the encircling gloom. We must rise early if we are to see her. If we discipline ourselves, however, we will find her.

Wisdom is bright, and does not grow dim.
    By those who love her she is readily seen,
and found by those who look for her . . .
Watch for her early and you will have no trouble;
    you will find her sitting at your gates. (Wisd.
    6:12–15)
The sage, though a 'mortal man', rose early and met
the Lady Wisdom,

And so I prayed, and understanding was given me;
    I entreated, and the spirit of Wisdom came to
    me.
I esteemed her more than sceptres and thrones;
    compared with her, I held riches as nothing.
    (Wisd. 7:7–8)

So, Wisdom, God's muse, his partner in creation, his beloved, is both the learning of the sages and the Word from which they learn. And lastly, of course, God's Wisdom is his mighty Word which leaped from his heart to take flesh amongst us.

In the beginning was wisdom.
    Wisdom was with God.
Wisdom *was* God.
Wisdom was made flesh
and lived amongst us,
    and we saw his – her glory.

Wisdom is bright and does not grow dim. The darkness may not receive her but it cannot overcome her. It cannot extinguish her light, and herein lies our hope.

*   *   *

Having deliberately blurred the boundaries of my three sources of wisdom, I shall perversely separate them once more. Let us consider first, then, the wisdom of the Elders, and see what we can learn from them. I am tempted here to sit on the floor amongst a pile of books and search out my favourite nuggets of wisdom: gems like these lines from the *Tao te Ching*:

> The Tao that can be told is not the eternal Tao
> > The name that can be named is not the eternal name.
> The nameless is the beginning of heaven and earth.*

or this old Egyptian saying:

> God is hidden, no man knoweth his form,
> > No man has searched out his similitude.
> He is hidden to gods and men. He is a secret to all his creatures ...
> His names are without number.
> His names are many; no man knowest the number of thereof.†

I could quote pages and pages of such wisdom, from Philo to Denys, Augustine to Thomas Aquinas, from the Koran and the Gita, but this is not the place. What emerges from all these sages is what Bede Griffiths called his 'golden string', the thread which, if carefully followed, leads to Nowhere, deep into the Sinai fog, into the heart of the Mystery. As Philo discovered, we search for God

---

* From the *Tao te Ching* by Lao-Tzu (6th century BC).

† Quoted in B. Greene and V. Gollancz (eds.), *God of a Hundred Names*, Hodder & Stoughton 1975.

only to discover that he cannot be found: and yet, some-how, there is joy in the searching. This is the point where, if I could sing, I would burst into Gilbert and Sullivan's 'A paradox, a paradox, a most ingenious paradox.' Because that's what we're up against. While Moses talks of 'the Cloud on Sinai', R. S. Thomas of 'the void' and Eckhart of 'the Silent Desert', we are faced with equally learned, equally holy men and women who claim to 'know' Jesus as friend, God as lover and who can address him with the simplicity of this Breton fisherman:

Protegez moi, mon Seigneur,
    Ma barque est si petite,
Et votre mer est si grande.
(Protect me, Lord; my boat is so small and your sea is
    so big.)*

Here we have in essence the wisdom of the elder holy men: God is mystery, transcendent, beyond all knowing; yet he is also immanent, in everything, in me, in you, in my teddy bear, as close as the neck of my camel. Enough (though can one *ever* have enough?) of the wisdom of holy men!

Let us move now into the world of the secular, to the psychologists, the psychotherapists, to those whose calling it is to look into the minds and hearts of God's most complex creatures. I have all too little book learning in the field but have spent many years, off and on, in psychotherapy and have found it more spiritually and humanly enriching than anything else I have done. How else would I have learned the amazing processes of devel-opment of the child, of the power of affectional bonds

* Quoted in *God of a Hundred Names.*

and the havoc wrought when they are ruptured? Where else but in my own flesh would I have learned the pain of betrayal when a trusted, adored adult strikes a small child? It is only in these very recent years that I have begun to understand something of the way in which parents and the society which mould them can sow seeds of violence in the hearts of children which may later flower into monstrous deeds. How can we not revise our ideas of sin and wickedness when we learn of the way in which child abuse so often begets abusers and how those deprived of love in childhood may never learn to love as healthy men and women should?

Surely, then, if we are to be privy to that secret earthquake of anguish that erupts in the souls of the dying, we should understand something of the ways of the minds and hearts God created? Sometimes the truth is hard to bear. How it must sear the heart of a priest to hear of abuses by one of his brother priests; how much easier to pretend that this is a wicked fantasy of a perverted imagination. How many years, I wonder, did Freud put back the understanding of child abuse when he did his famous *volte face* and decided that the painfully revealed memories of his clients' early years were merely erotic fantasies?

The sad thing, of course, is that all too often people abuse or are abused in ignorance. Surely those religious who were so harsh on the pupils in their care had no conception of the psychic damage they were inflicting, just as my father who beat me for being rude to an important visitor would have been horrified to know that I would remember it in terrifying detail fifty years on. Oh, God forgive us, for we know not what we do.

Perhaps the most important lesson I have learned from my years of therapy is the healing power of non-judgemental listening. Carl Rogers* speaks of UPR (unconditional positive regard), the kind of listening attention that provides a 'safe space' in which the client, the patient, the penitent, can unload the burden of frustration, anger, guilt and shame in his or her heart. That 'safe space' is like the mother's breast, like God's lap on to which one climbs in order to weep and to beg not only for forgiveness but for the power to forgive. Why, oh why, I wonder, do we feel so called upon to judge one another! Why can we not leave that to God, as Jesus told us: 'Judge not, and you will not be judged'? When will we hoist this on board?

It is, I believe, vitally important that those of us who are charged with the care of vulnerable people not only work towards deepening our understanding of our patients' psychological distress but make sure we are not seduced by those who would try to discredit such learning. I find a sad tendency among some people to mock social workers, probation officers and the like who look for the roots of sick behaviour. I do not believe that the world is full of wicked people – just a great many who are very wounded. The wisdom of the elders of our day is a gift from God and we must let it inform our own understanding.

The second of our sources of knowledge about God is what I have called the Wisdom of the Word: the Wisdom of the Scriptures, old and new. Since I write as a Christian and for Christians, I shall speak only of the scriptures from the Judeo-Christian tradition. This does not mean, however, that I am unaware of the richness of the holy writings of other faiths (I have placed them, somewhat

* In *On Becoming a Person*, Constable 1974.

arbitrarily, in the previous section). My own familiarity with the Old and New Testaments has grown steadily over the past fifteen to twenty years. I am not, to my shame, a regular reader of the scriptures (except perhaps the psalms), but I drink deeply in fits and starts. My real introduction to the scriptures happened at Ampleforth Abbey during a glorious eighteen months when I was allowed to pretend I was a monk and live on the monastery campus. I went, as good monks do, to the Divine Office several times a day and both sang the psalms and listened to the scriptures being read. It is difficult to explain to those who have never experienced it how different I found the listening to the Word of God in the monastery. There is something very powerful in listening to the scriptures in the company of twenty or thirty other people each of whom is listening with a seriousness and intensity quite different to that of an ordinary Sunday congregation. Now that I am once again an ordinary, rather restless and often reluctant attender at Sunday mass, I too am frequently deaf to the readings. Sometimes they are poorly delivered, but more often my mind wanders and as we sit for the sermon (hoping that it will not be too long), I wonder what on earth was the Gospel about? How *can* I have forgotten it already?

The greatest scriptural gift I received at Ampleforth, however, was from my friend Bonaventure, a gentle, rather disorganized monk with a deep knowledge and a passionate love of the Bible who gave me scripture tutorials each week. Dear Bon! How else would I have learned about the fire of prophets, fallen in love with Isaiah, puzzled about the meaning of 'the Kingdom' or been mind-boggled by the beauty of the Wisdom literature? It was Bon who taught me how to follow themes in the Bible, so that I can now undertake our magical journeys on my own, moving from John to Wisdom to Proverbs – and back again, picking up the echoes and the ideas, becoming so familiar with them that they become my own.

When I left Ampleforth in 1978 I went to 'try my vocation' in a women's monastery. The eighteen months I spent there were not particularly happy ones, for I am ill-suited to community life, but they were rich in familiarity with the Word of God. Women in a monastery have no houses to decorate, no dinner parties to host, no husbands to love. They do not go window-shopping or wonder which colours to wear today, what earrings will adorn them, whether or not to buy a new outfit. Their rhythms are different, marked not so much by the seasons of the year as by the Church's liturgical cycle. Perhaps you have to be stripped of ordinary pleasures to understand the amazing joy that the beauty of the Advent or Easter liturgy brings.

When I spoke earlier of my 'love affair' with Isaiah I meant it. My pulse quickened as we began the Advent readings, and my heart would soar as I heard Isaiah 9, 'The people that walked in darkness . . .', or Isaiah 11, 'A root shall spring from the stock of Jesse . . .' I illustrated the former with a fifty-foot frieze done on shelf paper, a long and motley crowd of the poor, the halt and the lame walking from the darkness of oppression towards the light of Christ. My contribution to the decoration of the refectory was graciously received but I suspect that the sisters got heartily sick of my hunted, hungry, people as they looked accusingly at any nun who dared to enjoy her leftover turkey!

This early monastic 'pickling' in the Word has stood me in good stead, for when I left the convent I was able to accept invitations to broadcast or preach and knew how and where to find a scriptural basis from which to teach. Sometimes I wish I had a theology degree, but I suspect that I have more fun as a dabbler and that hours of compulsory essay writing might kill my joy.

The other way in which I have been drawn to the Word has been through my contact with the Jesuits and through making individually guided Ignatian retreats. Since 1980 I have gone each year, sometimes three or four times, to be alone with God for a few days. This is the way that I personally 'cash out' my desire to be 'obedient' to God. By deliberately leaving behind my work, my novels, the TV and going away from home to a retreat house I plunge myself into silence and open my heart to listen. Each day I see the person who 'directs' me (accompanies me during the retreat), and he gives me two or three passages of scripture upon which to reflect. His choice is partly intuitive, governed by what I have told him and how he perceives my needs. I know that he is not infallible but I know too that if I accept what he gives me with open mind and heart they will 'speak' to my condition and that I will somehow meet God in them.

There are many different ways of listening to the Word of God. In *lectio divina*, the traditional monastic way of praying the scriptures, we read slowly, phrase by phrase, staying pensively with what strikes us and moving gently on when we have gained what we can. In 'imaginative contemplation', an Ignatian approach to seeking God's word, we try to enter into a particular passage, being present as the characters in a story are present, 'seeing', 'hearing', and allowing ourselves to be 'touched' by the story, by the event, by the Lord. I personally find it hard to do this so sometimes I draw the scene and 'experience' the word in a way which is quite different from *lectio divina*. I remember once drawing St Peter sitting outside Pilate's court, weeping bitterly at his betrayal. I looked at my sketch, poor as it was, and then found myself drawing Jesus walking past in chains on the way to Golgotha.

Peter's head remained bowed and his shoulders heaved: until Jesus sat beside him on the bench and put his arm around him to comfort him. I knew then how much Jesus loved Peter: and how much he loved me, in spite of my endless weak betrayals of him.

In this way, little by little, I have come to know the scriptures and in doing so have come to know God. My knowledge is patchy; I am more familiar with the Old Testament than the New and woefully ignorant of Paul's epistles. But I know there is time and that there are riches yet in store for me.

The last couple of years I have been absorbed in a new way of looking at the scriptures, exploring them for different images of God. In my searching I have uncovered an amazing wealth of imagery, different ways of picturing, trying to understand the Divine. I believe that this variety of images of God is not only intellectually fascinating but pastorally enormously important, because how can we talk to people about God if we do not know which God they worship? I am working at the moment with a lady who is a devout Jehovah's Witness. Her faith is impressive, although I personally cannot share her conviction that God would be angered if she accepted the blood transfusion she so badly needs. For her, this is clearly right, but if my idea of God was as inflexible as hers I would be ill equipped to minister to people whose understanding of God was different. As my own understanding of the Divine widens I find it easier to adapt to other people's language and beliefs and I hope that this makes me gentler and more compassionate. I would like to explore, now, some of these different understandings of God and how they might influence the way we work with the dying.

Loving the Old Testament as I do, it makes me both sad and exasperated that so many people, particularly those of an older generation, have been raised with the idea of God as a disapproving old man with a long white beard. This imagery brings out the iconoclast in me and I long to shatter their idols. Perhaps this is the danger of religious art; it leads us to take our anthropomorphic images so seriously that we forget that they are *only* images which should be blurred out again the moment they are painted. The trouble with these stereotyped images is that people connect the old man in the painting with some miserable old gentleman of their own acquaintance and decide, subconsciously, that God is like that. Who else (we are tempted to think) would be so demanding about going to boring church services on Sunday or so lacking in understanding of how lovers feel on a warm summer's night?

Perhaps the God who emerges in the early pages of the book of Job is partly to blame. What most people forget, however, is that the God of the great court of heaven who discourses with Satan and allows him to bait Job like a little boy pulling the wings off flies is in reality a panto-mime God, a story-book character used to make a point. The real God is the one Job meets on that dark and wonderful night when Yahweh answers him from the heart of the storm. The God who 'appears' there is a mysterious God, the God of Sinai, El Shaddai, the all-powerful, unnameable Creator God who is both scarily way 'out there' and marvellously, comfortingly, within us. He is the God of the mystics, the God of paradox.

Another of the common anthropomorphic images is that of Father. Jesus spoke all the time about his Father, the loving protector who both chastizes and forgives his children. This is a much gentler image, and clearly very helpful for many people. It is important, however, that we are wary of using the God as Father imagery with those whose experience of fathering has been less than satisfactory. Those who come from homes where mothers are warm loving figures and fathers strong gentle protectors sometimes forget that some parents are not so kind. Some fathers are cruel, some abuse their children, sexually or in other, more subtle ways. The children of such parents do not find the image of God as father helpful.

Sometimes the old images need only a little reinterpreting to be helpful. God as shepherd, for example, has little power these days, but if we think of the shepherd as the one who accompanies his creatures, his people, through dark and dangerous places, then perhaps the priest, counsellor or psychotherapist, familiar with the terrifying precipices of the mind, is the modern shepherd. I have spoken before of the holiness and power of non-judgemental listening, and I believe that this is one of the most important ways in which we can be Christ to each other.

The imagery which I find personally helpful is that of God as spouse. I love the concept of the *hesed* of God, his covenant faithfulness to us through thick and thin:

> for the mountains may depart
> > the hills be shaken,
> but my love for you will never leave you. (Isa. 54:10)

says Isaiah's God, and I believe him. I see a reflection of this covenant love all around me in the faithfulness of elderly men to their demented wives with Alzheimer's disease and in women tending their handicapped children or brain-damaged teenagers. Mine is the God of Isaiah, of Hosea and the Song of Songs. I am familiar with the God who pursues his distracted and unfaithful bride into the desert of prison, convent or depression and leads her weeping back home.

Perhaps at this point I should explain more clearly what I mean by these 'images' of God. What works for me are these word images which are related to but not the same as the pictures which they may conjure up. When I speak of the bridegroom pursuing his bride into the desert, I am not visually imagining God as a man driving, riding or walking along a dry and dusty road. No. I am saying that God's fidelity may be likened to that of the forgiving husband, the loving, patient old man, the passionate lover. Biblical images, as with all poetic language, must be allowed to slip lightly through the fingers, like a sunbeam or a rainbow.

> He who binds to himself a joy,
>> Doth the winged life destroy.
> But he who kisses the joy as it flies,
>> Lives in Eternity's sunrise. (William Blake)

The glorious thing about the Old Testament imagery is that it ranges from the most domestic, heart-warming anthropomorphic images – 'remember how I carried you in the desert, as a father carries his child' – to a shimmering array of abstract ones. I personally find the abstract imagery much easier to live with: God is light, he is the luminous, ethereal glow of moonlight on the dark sea, the blazing heat of the sun, the flicker of a candle as I sit praying in a darkened room. He is wind, spirit, breath, *ruah*, the power of life that quietly slips out of the child dying in his mother's arms. He is the unseen tempest that batters on my seaward windows during a winter storm:

> let in the wind,
> let in the rain,

let in your love tonight.*

Gerard Manley Hopkins, amazing wounded poet that
he was, found God everywhere: in the lush fecundity of
spring, in the wild skates–sweep of a circling wind hover
and in the warm hush of night as she settles broodingly
over a city composing itself for sleep. It was in his 'immortal diamond' image, however, that I found the key which
unlocked my understanding of divine imagery:

> Across my foundering deck shone
> A beacon, an eternal beam. Flesh fade, and mortal trash
> Fall to the residuary worm; world's wildfire, leave but
> ash:
>> In a flash, at a trumpet crash,
> I am all at once what Christ is, since he was what I am,
> and
> This Jack, joke, poor potsherd, patch, matchwood,
> immortal diamond,
>> Is immortal diamond.†

I saw Hopkins' diamond as one of those crystals that
are set on a revolving pedestal in a jeweller's window. As
the table slowly turns, the light catches the different facets
of the crystal so that it sparkles with a rainbow of colours.
I discussed this one day with poet Jim Cotter, and he said,
'Yes, we must let the crystal turn, because if we become
fixed on any one facet, any one image, it becomes idol-
atry.' We must let God reveal himself as and when he will,

* Kathleen Raine, from 'The Northumbrian Sequence', *Col-
lected Poems of Kathleen Raine*, Hamish Hamilton 1965.

† Gerard Manley Hopkins, from 'That Nature is a Heraclitean
Fire and of the Comfort of the Resurrection'.

as darkness or light, as presence or as absence, as tempest or gentle breeze. In short, we must let God be God.

The pragmatic, pastoral value of being able to 'sit lightly' to a variety of images of God means that we should be able to move more freely among people whose understanding of the divine is very different from our own without doing violence to them or ourselves. The question arises, of course, of what we should do with those who have what seems to us to be a very wrong image of God. By this I mean those who see God as heartless judge or manipulatory puppeteer: or, more common among religious people, those who see God as a sort of Santa Claus, a soft Daddy-figure who can be manipulated by the skilful to stay his hand or be good to his favoured few. I get quite hot under the collar when I meet those who believe that God can be bribed by the pious to cure his 'friends', i.e. his faithful servants. Where, I ask, does that leave the lady in the next bed who has no one to pray for her? I cannot and will not believe in a partisan God who gives knighthoods to those who have given a big donation to the party. My God is a foolish, big-hearted, untidy God who, if he has any preference at all, has a predilection for the *anawim*, the dispossessed, his little people.

Now for the last of the three ways in which we acquire knowledge of God – the wisdom of God herself. (I write 'herself' partly to bait the conservative, partly to keep my anti-sexist proofreader at bay but more than anything to state that I haven't a clue whether God is masculine, feminine, neither or both; nor do I care. God is God – totally other, beyond all knowing, yet deep in my heart.) I believe that the most important route to a knowledge of God, a working theology, is through prayer. We can read all the pious books in the world, but unless we sit silently at God's feet, open our minds and hearts to him, we will never really know him. This *knowing*, of course, is not an ordinary knowing. I don't know God like I know my boss, or my best friend. I don't know what he looks like. I've never seen him face to face. Like R. S. Thomas, I meet him mostly in his absences, entering rooms which he has just left, finding his prints on the dew-covered grass, or glimpsing him as he slips away between the trees. Forgive me if I resort to poetic imagery again; it's the only language I know for talking about God. I know God as faithful, because in my relationship with him he has been faithful to me. I know him as shepherd because he has somehow held my elbow as I have walked terrified along the edges of ravines. I have met him in a Chilean retreat house when I gave him my life as a blank cheque, and then in solitary confinement when I almost took it back. I 'know him' in the way of unknowing prayer and by realizing how he has been present in the crooked trajectory of my life. I can't explain it any better than that. If you are someone who prays you will know what I mean, and if you aren't, perhaps you should try.

Very occasionally, if I am faithful to prayer and listening, my understanding of God and his ways makes a sort of leap forward, so that I gain fresh insight and enthusiasms. These insights are not the fruit of study but of some intuitive creative process in which heart and mind work together to produce ideas. One such insight came to me in the night when I was on retreat in Birmingham last year. I had been given two passages of scripture to reflect on – Isaiah 55 and John 4, the story of Jesus and the Samaritan woman. Let me quote a few verses of the Isaiah:

> Oh, come to the water all you who are thirsty;
> > though you have no money, come!
> Buy corn without money, and eat,

and at no cost wine and milk.
Why spend money on what is not bread,
Your wages on what fails to satisfy?
Listen, listen to me, and you will have good things to
    eat
and rich food to enjoy.
Pay attention, come to me;
    listen and your soul will live. (Isa. 55:1–3)

Now this was a quite familiar passage for I had heard
it many times in monastic and parish liturgies, but I
turned my attention to it once more, as befitted a docile
retreatant. (One simply does not say to one's director, oh,
I *know* that one! How about something new?) After I had
mulled over the Isaiah I read the passage from John 4,
the familiar story of Jesus' encounter with the much-
despised, many-husbanded Samaritan lady at the well.
After Jesus had asked her for a drink the woman said to
him,

'What! You are a Jew, and you ask me, a Samaritan, for
a drink!' Now Jesus, who might well have said, 'Why ever
not?' or all sorts of comforting non-racist, non-sexist
things to make her feel good, said: 'If you only knew what
God is offering and who it is that is saying to you: Give
me a drink, you would have been the one to ask, and he
would have given you living water' (John 4:10).

As so often happens, I read the passage through several
times and nothing particular struck me. It's nice, I
thought. I like the living water image, it ties in with Moses
in the desert and all those bolshie, thirsty Israelites.
Having done my humble best I left it to lie fallow and
went to bed. Although not always a good sleeper I am not
given to nocturnal vigil-keeping so it was with singular ill
grace that I heaved myself from my bed at around 2 a.m.
that morning when I felt that God was somehow calling

me to pray. As I sat there, huddled in a blanket and blinking miserably at my candle, I 'heard' fragments of the two scripture passages in my head. 'O come to the water! Come! Come!' said the voice with enormous intensity. 'Listen! Listen to me!' I listened and then I 'heard' Jesus' phrase, 'If *only* you knew.' It was that 'only' that got me. If only I knew what? And then I realized what it was: it was God's love for us.

It sounds so trite and pious to say it like that. I have no words to express the power of that experience. I felt sick with grief. I felt hollow and I wept, because somehow I had caught a glimpse of the unrequited love of God for his people. It was then that I 'saw' the wheelchair. I saw that God is powerless, like someone physically handicapped. He sits, hunched up with loneliness and longing, wanting, wanting to tell his people how much he loves them, but he cannot cross the room, go up the stairs to tell them. He is like a cripple unable to join his friends at a party because there is no wheelchair access to the house where they are dancing, and no one comes to carry him up the steps. As I 'watched' the figure in the wheelchair I realized that someone must speak for him, be his messenger. Then I remembered the story of the call of Isaiah in Isaiah 6 and, in answer to God's 'whom shall I send?' I found myself saying, 'Send me! Send me!' I said. 'I know I'm pretty useless and I swear like a trooper, but if I'm any use, please send me!'

This, then, is how I see the pastoral care of the afflicted. They need not just physical and emotional care, understanding and forgiveness, but they need to know that God loves them. They need to know, moreover, the passion and the tenderness with which he loves and there is no one but us to take this message to them. We must be his hands, his lips, his voice, and we must deliver his message in a form that they can understand. Mostly, this means that we must not so much *say* how much God loves people but *reveal* to them that they are lovable. By treating people with all our skill, compassion and love we are revealing to them that they are infinitely precious, that they are worthy of love. Sometimes this is all that we can do to tell people of God's love for them, for if a person has no faith he or she will not understand us however ardently we speak about God. At other times, of course, our stumbling words will find a home in someone's heart. These words must always be tempered to understanding of the person we are speaking to, but above all they must come from our own heart, from our own personal store of lived knowledge. This is why it is so vital that pastors should be men and women who pray, who 'know' God, for how else can we speak with authority, give hope to those who would otherwise despair?

9

Some Thoughts on Euthanasia

EVERY TEN DAYS or so I get a letter in a childish hand saying, 'Dear Doctor Cassidy, I know you are very busy but ... I have to do a project on euthanasia for my religious studies ...' There follows a request for answers to questions or material on mercy killing. As I read the letter I sigh and consign it to my 'pending' tray and vow I must get myself better organized for such requests.

Curiously enough, even in the present climate, the euthanasia question is not high on my personal agenda. My days are filled with medical, human and personal problems, but whether or not to kill my patients is not an issue – quite simply, I don't. I don't kill my patients, all of whom are terminally ill, because mostly they do not want to be executed, and because I believe that 'mercy killing' is murder and therefore against the law of God and of man. I am, therefore, firmly against the legalization of euthanasia and, should it become legal, I shall still refuse to practise it.

I would like to say how I see things from where I stand – from the bedside of the terminally ill rather than from the moral theologian's armchair. If my language is distressingly earthy, please remember that I write of medical reality, not theological theory. My purpose is not so much to give words to my irritation as to clarify some of the ambiguities about what is and is not euthanasia, so as to reduce the rising level of anxiety among ordinary non-medical people.

Let me begin with the commonest myth: that our hospitals are full of men and women dying in terrible agony and begging the hard-hearted doctors to put them out of their misery. This just is not so. Throughout Britain doctors and nurses are doing their level best to control the pain and distress of the terminally ill. Granted, it is not always easy, and there is still much room for improvement, but great efforts are being made to teach good terminal care to all health-care professionals.

Not only is there now a hospice in virtually every major city but there are over 140 hospital support teams in which specialist doctors and nurses are on call to assist and advise those caring for the terminally ill. The Cancer Relief Macmillan Fund, more power to its elbow, is supporting such teams all over the United Kingdom.

Having said this, it is important to admit that we do not completely eradicate all pain, though we can virtually always reduce it to manageable levels. Should some hypothetical pain be impossible to subdue, there always remains the possibility of pain control allied with sedation.

From time to time, patients do ask us to end their suffering. If a patient asks me to kill him I would listen very closely; it would be very wrong to brush away such a courageous and awesome request. It is important to elucidate precisely why someone wishes to die: is he clinically (i.e. medically, chemically) depressed, for example, or distressed at feeling a burden on relatives or carers? Many terminally ill patients do become depressed and respond well to antidepressant therapy. Others feel better when they realize that their carers love and cherish them, however weak and broken. There does, however, remain a small core of people who find their debilitated and dependent state intolerable, and to these patients I would offer sedation, asking, 'Would you like to be more sleepy most of the time?' If they *would* like this, we would prescribe regular sedative drugs, achieving a level of sedation that allows the patient to be woken for care and nourishment, and then drift off to sleep again. It sometimes happens that such people sleep their lives away over a few weeks or days – but I am clear that here the primary intention is the relief of emotional distress, not the ending of the person's life.

We have learned as a team that one must be very clear that it is the patient's wish to be sleepy and not the relatives or the carers longing for them to be 'at peace'. I well remember a lady we cared for who had a destructive cancer of her maxillae, her cheekbones. The tumour had completely eaten away her nose and one eye and blinded the other so that there was only a foetid gaping hole where her face had been. We longed for her to die – she seemed so dehumanized, and we sedated her to 'keep her comfortable' until her nurse came to us and said she was fighting through the haze of the sedation. When we found that she had no desire to lie down peacefully to comfort us, we stopped the drugs and she got up and played the piano, blind and disgusting and disfigured as she was. The human spirit is a very remarkable thing and not all those we wish out of the way want to go.

But what about 'passive' euthanasia, the non-administration of life-saving drugs or the withdrawal of life-support systems? When I was a young medical student struggling with medical ethics, we were taught Clough's rhyme:

> Thou shalt not kill; but need'st not strive
> Officiously to keep alive.

I reckon that is as clear a guideline as most of us need (even though Clough did not mean it that way). If an old man with lung cancer, thin and weary with coughing and general debility, longing for it all to be over, gets a chest infection we would think twice about treating it. If the infection makes him more distressed, then of course we would give him antibiotics. But often pneumonia, the 'old man's friend', sets in within a few hours and death comes speedily and mercifully. Such a patient, were he not terminally ill, could be treated vigorously with intravenous antibiotics and a respirator, but such treatment would be meddlesome in the elderly or the dying.

How actively we treat people depends upon each individual patient's situation and in particular upon his personal relationships. Sometimes a couple, of whatever age, are so in love that each day of even seemingly poor-quality life is of inestimable value. They fight bravely for each bonus day and we fight with them with whatever means are at our disposal. I believe it will always be thus, and no financial cuts will deny treatment to those who want it and who will benefit from it. This last phrase is very important, because very often dying people and their families clutch so violently at straws that their carers can be tempted to accede to their desperate pleas and administer useless treatment. This, I believe, is unethical, especially if the treatment is 'invasive' so that it has unpleasant side-effects.

It is important for the lay person to understand the difference, as medical people see it, between ordinary and 'extraordinary' means of treatment. If a person is unable to eat or drink because his brain is damaged, then he will die. He will die of the primary disease, which has rendered him incapable of taking nourishment. Now when someone has a stroke or a head injury, we have no immediate means of knowing whether or not he has the potential to recover, whether the brain disease is reversible. Such patients are therefore kept alive by *extraordinary* means, by intravenous infusions or tubes down their noses and into their stomachs. They must be turned every two hours if they are not to get terrible bed sores and their bowels are cleared by digital removal of faeces from the rectum. All this is very intensive and invasive nursing. It is life-saving in those patients whose brain damage is transitory. But it is not an *ordinary* way to nurse people and it is not appropriate to continue it indefinitely in those patients with irreversible brain damage.

I do not believe, therefore, that it was a step along the path to euthanasia when a court permitted a hospital to stop the life-support machine which had kept a brain-damaged young man alive in a vegetative for many months. I believe it is an intelligent, humane and Christian way to treat a person whose body has been so badly damaged that it can no longer sustain life. I do not for one moment think that such legislation will lead to the quiet extermination of old ladies with Alzheimer's disease or the congenitally handicapped. By the grace of God (and it really is the grace of God) there are nurses who feel called to do the ordinary caring tasks for the elderly and the profoundly handicapped. They willingly wash and feed and love the feeble of brain, spooning custard patiently into aimless mouths and talking lovingly to those who never answer. Such care is right and proper – for it is *ordinary* caring and involves no tubes, no respirators and no high-tech medicine.

I sometimes wish that the theologizers would not talk of doctors and nurses as if they were longing to dispatch their more tedious clients and find someone or something more entertaining to treat. Those of us who work day by day with the terminally or chronically ill are quite clear where we stand; we are called to work with broken people, accompanying them lovingly and professionally along the way to their death. We have no mandate to expedite that death, however longed for, but neither do we feel obliged to prolong life for the sake of it. Death comes to all of us, either as friend or foe, and our task is to fight it for as long as people wish and we are able, and then, quite simply, to *be there* when it comes.

If euthanasia were legal, however, or even sort-of-legal, as in Holland, then I believe that a lot of sick and elderly people would feel obliged to do the 'decent thing' by their families and ask to be 'put to sleep'. What the dying fear even more than pain and indignity is being a burden. And they fear being a burden because, like all of us, they are terrified of rejection. People, all people when they are grievously ill, are vulnerable to losing their sense of personal worth, to feeling useless, fit for nothing. But Christianity has a clear reassurance for them: you are worth more than many sparrows because God your father made you and because he loves you. He loves you now, today, and perhaps more than ever before if you are old and sick and daft and incontinent, because is he not a paradoxical God who seeks out the lost sheep and loves the *anawin*, the little people?

It is this same God who calls doctors and nurses and social workers to care for his widows and orphans, his blind, his sick and his broken-hearted; he has always called such people and I believe he always will. And if we have skilled and loving carers to look after the sick, to reveal the face of God to them, who needs euthanasia?

10

The Cost of Caring

ALTHOUGH THE TITLE of this last 'essay' has been pushing its way insistently into my mind for some time, now that I come to put pen to paper I am not quite sure just what it is that I want to say. A couple of weeks ago a younger doctor sat quietly in the ward office while I was letting off steam about – well, never mind what about – and, in answer to my unprintable comments, she grinned and said, 'You say it like it is, don't you?' Slightly surprised I grinned back and agreed. Perhaps, then, this is as good a place as any to start: the cost of speaking out and the cost of keeping quiet.

Let's look first at the question of speaking out. The modern Latin American prophets speak about being 'the voice of the people who have no voice', and it seems to me that this is one of the most important ways in which we incarnate the gospel. The trouble is, however, the truth is not always welcomed by those who need to hear it. It's one thing to speak the truth in a general sort of way, without naming names. I do a lot of that when I teach, trying to alert doctors and nurses to the ways in which we can unwittingly hurt those for whom we are trying to care. I'm sure this is a worthwhile exercise and I believe that, in the last ten years, the 'hospice philosophy' has had a profound effect upon hospitals all over the country. It is, however, a very different thing to go to a colleague and

[115]

say, in effect, 'You did that wrong,' or, 'You handled that patient badly.' There are three issues here: charity, courage and pragmatism. The better I get to know my working colleagues, the more I respect them and the more I like them. They, like me, are flawed human beings trying to achieve a reasonable balance between honest work and personal survival. If I go to one of these men or women and say, 'You upset Mrs X,' or, 'Mrs Y thinks you're an arrogant B,' the chances are that not only will I hurt them deeply but I will alienate myself from them altogether. The converse, however, is if we think that what we're doing is fine when it isn't, how will we ever learn to do it differently? There is yet another side to this; it can be extremely painful and humiliating to find out that people have been unhappy about some aspect of one's behaviour for months or even years and yet have never had the courage to say so. I know that I have been very angry when this has happened to me and yet I know too that I don't have the courage to 'speak the truth in love' to others. The third issue is that so often it is politically 'dangerous' to speak out. Juniors who are outspoken to their bosses may not get references and any would-be prophet is readily seen as a trouble-maker. The real issue is that it's often very difficult to know what is the right thing to do and this uncertainty causes unhappiness and conflict: and this is what I mean by the 'cost of caring'.

The other cost, of course, is when someone else has the courage to tell *you* that you've got it wrong; and if you thought you were doing fine that really hurts. The first reaction may be to fight back, or to go away and sulk, or just burst out crying. I, to my eternal shame, cope very badly with criticism, usually perceive it as rejection and weep uncontrollably. This has happened to me several times during the past year, and I find it all the more painful because my *perception* of myself is that I am open-minded and willing to learn and would really like to be corrected!

Whether we like it not, however, mechanisms are being set up so that we may learn from our mistakes. 'Medical audit', the systematic examination of our practice and its results, is here to stay. Part of me hates the whole business, but the wiser woman sees that this must be good.

The other mechanism for fraternal correction is team meetings. O Lord, how I hate meetings, but I know how vital they are, particularly in small hot-house units like hospices where jealousies and rivalries can flourish like bindweed, choking out healthy growth. I think, as I write, of Jesus' story of the wheat and the darnel. What, I wonder, was he saying? Perhaps it is that we are all made up of wheat and darnel, so that if you try to root out one you will end up pulling them all and be left with a barren field. One of the things I have learned in the process of growing up is that my weaknesses are the flip side of my strengths. The artist in me is wildly creative and I am full of splendid ideas and enthusiasm. This is all very fine, but my artistic child is singularly messy and leaves a trail of belongings wherever it goes. Clothes, books, paper, unwashed coffee cups are a sure sign that Sheila has been playing here and has moved on to a more exciting game. It is not for nothing that I sometimes describe myself as coming from a long line of artistic sluts! My other great difficulty is in time-keeping. I am a cheerful optimist, ever convinced that I can cram just one thing more into the unforgiving minute, and am therefore frequently late. I know in my heart that punctuality is the politeness of princes but, however hard I try, I seem always to be defeated, arriving last of any group with a breathless excuse about the traffic or that last-minute phone call.

It will come as no surprise to anyone who works in a community setting that the greatest stress in working with the dying is caused not by contact with the patients and their families but with colleagues and governors. Before I go any further, let me say that my relationship with colleagues at work has also been a source of enormous joy to me. I have worked with the same group of women (yes, women, for it is rare for us to have more than one or two men among a staff of over fifty) for more than ten years and many of them have become my close friends. What, then, goes wrong? I'm not sure, in fact, if anything goes 'wrong'; it's just that working closely with people is costly. What is perhaps peculiar to hospices, however, is that we are all trying so hard to be perfect! Hospices have set themselves the impossible task of trying to be all things to all men and women. We are used to death, God help us, but our patients are not. This is the first time for them, and they are very frightened. They don't know the 'rules of the game': that it's all right to weep for yourself, but that it's not OK to be horrid to the lady in the next bed, however much she may irritate you. Families, too, are stretched to screaming point; mothers-in-law fall out with sons-in-law and teenage girls get bolshie and slam doors. Wives lie to protect their husbands and stand guard like tigresses, bottle-brush tails erect, lest any interfering doctor or nurse should tell their man that he's going to die and therefore make him 'give up'. All this, of course, we take in our stride, but it costs. Then there are the young mothers who lie there and cry and cry that they want to see their little daughters grow up and we sit there impotent, hearts raging against God, against fate and against their feckless husbands who can't bring themselves to love and honour their frail wives for just a few more weeks until death sets them free. We, poor fools, because we have learned all about fear and anger and loss and alienation in our patients, think that we can heal their pain but we can't. And – because *we* can't burst into tears and say, 'What the hell do you expect *me* to do? I'm not God. I'm only human and frankly, right now, I'd rather be somewhere else' – we say something sharp to one of our colleagues instead, and they take it personally and ... and so it goes on.

How long can you work at what one psychiatrist calls 'the sharp end' of caring? Frankly, I don't know. I suspect it depends upon the individual and his or her support systems. I lecture a lot about 'occupational stress' in the care of the dying and have learned a little of the jargon. One useful phrase is 'person–environment fit'; that is, do I have the skills to cope with my job and does my job satisfy my needs? If the fit is close, that is, if I like my work, find it satisfying and am competent to do it, then I'll survive longer than someone for whom the fit is less exact. I'm lucky. I like sick people and I feel comfortable with people facing death. I'm reasonably good at diagnosing and sorting out the physical side of illness and I don't get screwed up when I can't cure someone. But there are other things I am not so good at. I'm very shy and hate a lot of the PR side of hospice work. I can lecture to a thousand people or appear endlessly on the TV, but ask me to go to a pub to receive a cheque or come to a staff party, then I'm a nervous wreck. *Chacun à son goût!*

The other side of hospice life which cost me dear was management. A hospital colleague said to me a few months ago, 'Everyone knows you're a terrible manager!' I was both surprised and hurt, because I've always tried to be a fair and generous team leader and thought I had succeeded. Perhaps I should have challenged my accuser, but I was too taken aback. On reflection, I think there are two styles of management: you can lead by consensus, or you can impose your rule without explanation. I have always tried to do the former because I despise the latter. But times are changing; resources are scarce and the health-care profession is being converted to a market place. I hate that side of health care, and while I try to use my resources carefully I have no heart for endless financial wheeler-dealing. I do not wish to haggle with the government for money or the health authority for contracts, so perhaps it's just as well that I've left the hospice.

The other words which make my blood pressure rise are 'council' or 'governors'. Hospices are, for the most part, charitable institutions, and this means that they are under charity law, set up as limited companies with a board of governors. The 'governors', 'council' or 'trustees' are the members of the 'board' who are responsible for the management of the hospice. The doctors, nurses, social workers, chaplain and administrator – the people who actually do the day-to-day running of the business – are employees of the hospice and responsible to the council. Now this should, in theory, be fine, and it often is; but it is fraught with possibilities for conflict. The senior employees of the hospice, while carrying the enormous professional responsibility of caring for desperately ill people and their families, have no place by right at meetings of the council of management. They sit there by invititation and can be asked to leave at any time. I do not doubt the good will or the hard work of our own or other trustees, but I have grave doubts about a system in which men and women completely untrained in the management of health professionals are given total power over a vulnerable institution and its workforce. Hospice councils are made up of volunteers: retired businessmen, busy solicitors, overworked doctors, senior nurses and clergymen, who often have neither the time nor the expertise to manage either wisely or justly. It will come as no surprise then, that, in a survey of causes of stress in hospice matrons and medical directors, conflict with the council of management came highest on the list of stressors.

I have thought quite a bit about hospice management during my eleven years at St Luke's. In that time I have seen council chairmen come and go and I have tried desperately to communicate with them like an adult human being. I have written papers, made phone calls, and been granted interviews, and somehow I have got it wrong. Perhaps it's me, or perhaps it's the system. One of my theories is that personality clashes between hospice staff and governors is almost inevitable because the two occupations draw such different personalities. If you are familiar with Myers–Briggs personality types, then I suspect that the sort of people who volunteer for and enjoy being trustees are pragmatic STJ types who have little sympathy with or time for vulnerable, intuitive, open-ended NFPs. What I'm trying to get at is this: I think you need different personal qualities to care for the dying than you need to run a business or be a successful nurse manager, a go-ahead solicitor or vicar of a large parish. Hospices tend to attract particularly vulnerable, intuitive, caring people who, having been hurt somewhere along the line themselves, are comfortable in the presence of the very wounded. Men and women who volunteer to sit on councils believe deeply in the ideals of care of the dying but often find themselves impatient of the frailties of those who actually do the work. A song from *My Fair Lady* goes: 'Why can't a woman be more like a man!' – and no doubt the council would chant in neat unison, 'Why can't *they* be more like *us*?'

I wish I knew what the answer is. Should hospices organize themselves like religious orders, *electing* their council of management from among the ranks of their members to *serve* the community for a fixed period of time? Should there be a career structure in hospice management, a sort of specialty in health service management? I find it amazing that hospital administrators are trained to manage but hospices are inclined to assume that a successful army officer or retired businessman will have the skills to manage their workforce without any special training. Enough!

Now that I have left the hospice and the yoke of responsibility has been lifted from my aching shoulders, I can see two other important 'costs' of working in that environment. The first and most important of these is the cost of working in a *multidisciplinary team*. For those for whom this is jargon, I am talking about an institution in which many of the hierarchical barriers between doctors and nurses have been broken down, so that the traditional medical pyramid with the senior doctor as an apical god and the doctors, social workers and nurses arrayed in polite ranks under his command is replaced by a team in which each discipline is not only represented but respected by the others. This way of working (would it be termed collegiality in ecclesiastical circles?) is integral to hospices and I believe in it passionately. I have learned over the years to respect and value my nurse, social work and administrative colleagues in a way that would have been impossible had I stayed within the hospital system. But, like all things, this way of working has its costs. I think that one of the things that happens is that we get to know each other almost too well; we become, in fact, a sort of family with all the good and the bad things that characterize family life. This means, I believe, that not only do we have to work at our relationships but we lose the protective distance that usually exists between professionals. I have for many years been fascinated by the working style of one of my senior colleagues at the hospital. He is an exceptionally reserved man, even-tempered and just, and I both trust and respect him deeply.

In the early years of our relationship I thought him a bit stuffy, one of the old school of doctors; over the years, however, I have come to see that his reserve enables him to stand clear of the various factions in departmental feuds and intrigues. Perhaps, I say to myself, there is something to be said after all for the rather formal rituals of behaviour that characterize relationships between staff in a big hospital. I suspect it is not unlike what happens in monasteries: perhaps I should reread St Benedict's Rule and see if it can be modified for use in hospices!

The other characteristic of hospice life that has an unseen cost is the fact that, as a charity, we are beholden to our supporters and must therefore mind our Ps and Qs rather more than our state-funded colleagues. Living in a goldfish bowl is not everyone's cup of tea, and I heave a great sigh of relief these days as I wander happily around the wards and corridors of our big general hospital and know that I shall not suddenly be plucked from my reverie and required to be nice to a group of ladies from the Inner Wheel or the Mothers' Union. It's not that I am not glad that the people of Plymouth and its environs support the hospice, but I do not feel personally or professionally indebted to them, for I believe that we are all grown-up people caring for a particular group of the vulnerable of our society. They care by fund-raising, I by working at the hospice. O Lord, what blasphemy am I talking! but I know I speak for many of the staff, for we revel in those quiet weekends when nothing more is asked of us than that we do our jobs with love and competence.

Another rather similar cost is that imposed by the professional visitor. This is a price I am more than willing to pay, for I know that people are hungry to learn and we want to share what we have learned. There is, none the less, a price to be paid in terms of energy for every disciple who comes to sit at our feet. St Benedict had quite a bit to say about visitors, adding wryly, 'for the monastery is never without them'. They should be welcomed, said Benedict, as 'Christ himself', and we *do* try but, like all families, we need some time to ourselves if we are to cherish the bonds which hold us together.

Enough about the costs of caring. No doubt some readers will quote the famous remark, 'If you can't stand the heat, get out of the kitchen!' Well, I have got out, but I staunchly reserve the right to reflect about the experiences of one-fifth of my life.

The last thing I would like to explore is the way in which I and those with whom I worked have managed to survive – what is known in professional jargon as our 'coping strategies'. The first thing that strikes me is this: if you don't have coping strategies then you won't survive. It's as simple as that. So, how does one go about learning these survival techniques? What do I have to teach those who find themselves on the hard road to burn-out?

Taking as read the need for a close person–environment fit, I think the next most important things are a sense of humour and a deep determination to squeeze as much fun as possible out of life. The third requirement is the ability to take all the time out that is legitimate, plus what my good friend Carolyn, the social worker, calls 'the occasional delinquency'! The fourth requirement is that we maintain that vital professional space between ourselves and the patients. Let me elaborate, first about the sense of humour. Death and dying is a very painful business, and so is being in constant proximity to those who are suffering in the process. As in all such situations, however, tragedy and farce are never very far apart and – like mortuary attendants, police and undertakers – we develop a chameleon-like ability to move from a stance of deep and genuine compassion to near hysterical laughter. My favourite hospice photo is of a group of social workers and doctors having lunch after we had moved the hospice from its cramped suburban home to its present glorious purpose-built palace overlooking the sea. Nearly every one's mouth is either crammed full of food or wide open with mirth; some of them (no names mentioned!) were both. The other memory is of the desperate lady who, emotionally exhausted by her husband's long-drawn-out passing, tried to encourage him on his way by telling that she could hear the gates of heaven opening and that their much loved but departed doggie was standing there, lead in mouth, waiting to be taken for a walk! The crash of heavenly gates, if I remember rightly, was either something falling off a trolley or, worse still, a patient falling out of bed!

What about the fun then? How do we manage that in the midst of such sadness without giving offence? Perhaps the greatest misconception about hospices is that they are solemn places populated by an alien race of people who have ceased to be part of the human race and their angelic dedicated carers. I suppose that's why so many people talk about 'them' or 'your residents' in hushed voices. I am always at pains to make clear that the dying are not *them* but *us*, men and women, pious or bawdy, kind-hearted or selfish, Guinness drinkers or tee-total. We die as we live, and we are alive until our heart stops beating. The patients, then, at least quite a proportion of them, get assimilated into our very motley family. They tease and get teased, they laugh and they cry and sometimes, for a few blessed minutes or hours, they forget that they are dying. I suspect that our patients love us most when, having acknowledged the enormity of their tragedy, we treat them like 'normal' people.

A lot of our fun, of course, goes on behind closed doors. We have a special 'Wednesday cake' each week at the team meeting and we talk endlessly about clothes. (Pity the poor vicar or occasional male doctor!). 'Can I have your clothes when you die, Dr Cassidy?' chant the auxiliary nurses as I sweep past in yet another glorious ethnic creation.

I've thought a lot about the clothes business, mostly because it makes me feel guilty that I spend so much money on myself. Not long ago I stumbled over the beginning of an essay which never came to anything and read the following:

> Last week I bought five sweaters. Five! One blue, one red, one green and two navy. Last week we had five deaths, one thirty, one forty-five, one twenty and two sixty-two. I wonder: is there any connection?

Of course there is a connection. If I pour myself out for the hungry and shelter the homeless poor, my light may rise in the darkness, but I also find myself exhausted, spent, empty. How, then, am I to refuel, to replenish that emotional energy and vitality which is the precious fuel on which I run? I have always longed to be the sort of person who recoups their energy by listening to classical music or reading highbrow novels; but I am not. What I *really* like is to go shopping! I love the excitement of the chase, the bubbling optimism that says that today is the day I shall find the skirt, the top, the trousers that will make me look slim and elegant and lovely and, not only that, it will also have 75 per cent knocked off the price! Then there's the colour. I love colour. It feeds something deep in my soul and I stand and absorb the colours of a row of Indian skirts as if I were sunbathing. There's something very special about natural dyes. I could roll on the floor in delight among the Persian carpets in my favourite shop, and if there was any more space on my floor I would go out immediately and buy another one!

Indigo is my favourite colour and I delight in buying clothes which have the following warning: 'this garment is guaranteed to turn you and your underclothes bright blue'! I remember ruefully the evening when I went to mass after dying a few shirts. Alas, I had forgotten to wear rubber gloves and my hands became irrevocably stained a deep bluish purple. I scrubbed them till the skin nearly came off but when I raised them piously to receive holy communion the priest looked aghast at them and shoved the host unceremoniously into my mouth. I was not amused: but then neither was he. I hope God was!

It's all very well for *you*, doctor, you will no doubt say. You earn a nice fat salary and you have no children to send to school, to camp, to music lessons. Ah well! we won't go into that one, but as I say to the nurses when they get too envious, 'Here am I, a poor lonely spinster with nothing but my designer woollies to keep me company. . . .'

Most fun, of course, are the 'occasional delinquencies', either gastronomic or sartorial. Both Carolyn and I have a terrible weakness for chocolate cake or rather that extravagant cross between cake and pudding which is known as 'Death by Chocolate', and our waistlines suffer accordingly. My other great source of comfort is the television. Each night when I arrive home I make a dive for the *Radio Times* and scan its pages anxiously. If one of my favourite detective thrillers or medical 'soaps' is on, my happiness is complete and I purr like a contented cat in the anticipation of another perfect evening.

I suppose it must sound a bit pathetic if an evening devoted to light-hearted TV is seen as perfect: but in the context of my life it is all I need. In the empty silence of the early morning I pray, opening my heart to God and the pain of his world. Then, girding my loins in Indian cotton and my ears with amber, mock jade or lapis lazuli,

I set out to do battle with Death. After nine or ten hours of fighting I've had enough. I am empty, poured out like water, my tongue cleaving to my palate and my bones broken. Then, like an exhausted animal, I creep back to my lair and, because I have no husband or lover to be good to me, I have learned to be good to myself. I feed my seagull who stands importunately at the kitchen window and then the evening is mine. I have learned to my cost that empty vessels need refilling, that I am only human, and perhaps that is why I survive.

It may seem strange that I have left the consideration of the cost of working with the patients themselves until last. I'm sure, however, that this order will seem perfectly logical to fellow hospice workers. The fact is, we are hardly ever to be heard moaning about our patients: it is always the council, the matron, the administrator, or just 'the system'. We often say we're busy or it's been a hard day, but we practically never *name* the clinical work as stressful. Why, I wonder, do we deny what everyone else can see – that this work is enormously costly? Perhaps we grieve so deeply for our people, are so enraged at the cruel fate that has befallen them, that it never occurs to us to 'blame' them for our own pain. Could it be that we even feel *guilty* for being well and free while they are sick and fettered? Who knows? I believe that we somehow repress our pain, partly because it is too great to acknowledge, partly because we are afraid of being seen as not 'coping' with the work. I used to protest vigorously that I didn't find my work painful, until one day I was at the theatre watching a play which included a deathbed scene. Suddenly, to my horror, I found myself sobbing (mercifully silently) with a grief that surprised and frightened me. On another occasion, while on retreat, I suddenly found myself weeping in anguish for one of my young patients who was dying a particularly slow and tiresome death. As

I said earlier, most of the time the pain is suppressed, but it comes out in the form of staff conflict, exhaustion or irritability with friends or family.

And what of 'burn-out'? *Do* hospice people burn out? Clearly some do, although I'm told that Dame Cicely Saunders doesn't believe in 'burn-out', only in 'battle fatigue'. Sometimes I dare to ask myself if I was 'burnt out' in my work at the hospice. I don't really know the answer. I know I was desperately weary of hospice politics, management and the endless financial issues. I know that I felt ill equipped for and impatient of the long-drawn-out meetings and the looming issues of contracts with the health authority. That yoke I was indeed glad to relinquish. But the actual clinical work, the care of the patients – was I burnt out on that? Frankly, I don't think so, because I am full of enthusiasm for the same work at the hospital. There is, however, one significant difference in my role at the hospital: although I do not carry over all responsibility for the patients I visit, I am the only palliative-care doctor that they see and I therefore have a very close relationship with them. At the hospice things were different because I was the senior doctor supervising three other doctors in their care. In that situation, it was they who became close to the patients, not me. This is an important issue because although the closer you are to the patient the more you share their pain, the closer you are, the more satisfaction you get from the work. Although we don't often talk about it, we need our patients as much as they need us, because we too need to be loved.

The last of my four coping strategies is that the carer should maintain a professional space between him- or herself and the patient or client. Before you write me off as another of those cool professionals who is afraid to get 'too involved' with their patients, let me explain. When I speak of maintaining a professional space I am talking about a mental exercise on the part of the carer: that is, that he or she never forgets that this person is *not* a personal friend or a relative but is a patient or a client. Most medical institutions are so arranged that there is no risk of their carers forgetting these things; the doctor in his white coat, seated behind the clinic desk and attended by nurses and receptionists, is very clear about his or her role. Hospice doctors and nurses, however, are much closer to their patients and their families; they will call them by their first names, be privy to their inmost secrets and, if they are similar in age or personality, may identify closely with them. This closeness is not a professional error; it is often the most precious thing we have to give to our people who are frequently lonely and isolated with a greatly diminished sense of personal worth. If, in the process of accompanying the dying, we become so close to them that we take too much of their pain upon ourselves, then we will be at risk of burn-out. If, however, we are very clear in our minds that this person is a patient, not a personal friend, then we can afford to become really close to them without getting personally hurt. Carl Rogers speaks of this in his book '*On Becoming a Person*' when he discusses empathy as one of the essential ingredients for growth in the therapeutic relationship. Empathy, says Rogers, is the ability to enter into the clients' world so that we can experience what they feel *as if* we were them, but without losing the *as if* quality. It is this hairline distinction which is the carer's salvation. So long as I am clear in my own mind that I am a doctor and my patients are patients, then I can befriend them, cherish them, hug them and allow them to hug me. If I was *not* thus clear, I would either distance myself from them for fear of being hurt or go under.

It is perhaps worth sharing a small piece of wisdom that

I have learned in my time at St Luke's. When I was young and insecure as a doctor I always wore my white coat and behaved with as much dignity and decorum as I could muster. That was in my previous existence when I was in the business of curing people. In terminal care, however, one has no such luxury. Much of the time I must work with my hands empty, drawing upon my own personal resources to comfort anguished patients. This means that I am often very informal with them. I have long since shed my professional façade because I now know that patients see right through such armour and what they really respect is that heady mixture, competence and compassion. Sometimes I think of myself like the wretched mother pelican, pulling the feathers out of my breast until the blood flows to feed my starving children. I believe that it is this drawing upon one's own resources that makes all the difference in the care of the terminally ill. The hospital specialist may legitimately say, 'I'm sorry, there is nothing more that I can do to help you.' Specialists in palliative care, however, must accept that the buck stops with them; they have made a covenant with their people to accompany them until they die. Like the Lord, whose hands they must be, they must say:

. . . the mountains may depart,
the hills be shaken,
but my love for you will never leave you
and my covenant of peace with you will never be shaken.
    (Isa. 54:10).